scandilicious
Baking

Signe Johansen

Photography
by Tara Fisher

In loving memory of
my grandmothers Juliet and Oddny,
great bakers both.

CONTENTS

Introduction

The smell of freshly baked bread or the rich scent of spice cake wafting from the kitchen – how enticing is that? Just the thought of it makes me happy. Of all the cooking I've done over the years, baking was the first kitchen skill I learned and is still my favourite. Home-made fruity muffins and sticky cinnamon bun-cake, flaky buttery pastries fresh from the oven, delicious chocolate cardamom biscuits to pop in pretty packaging and give to friends... You'll find all these in here and more.

Scandinavian baking covers a fantastically varied spectrum – from cakes, pastries and indulgent sweet treats to crusty breads, more-ish nibbles and mouthwatering savoury dishes, plus plenty of warming winter comfort food besides – and you'll find four key players making an appearance time and again throughout this book: grains, almonds, spices and seasonal fruit.

Grains – the Scandinavian baker tends to use not only wheat but also rye, barley, spelt and oats in sweet and savoury dishes. Rye features in dark chewy pumpernickel bread, crunchy granola and the pastry for classic dishes like Finnish Karelian pies. Barley grains make a fabulously creamy baked pudding and barley flakes are a great addition to your daily bread or flapjack bar. Spelt has a heritage dating back thousands of years as the forefather of modern wheat and you can use refined spelt flour instead of plain flour in many recipes. It makes great cakes and pastry, and many people find it more digestible too. Finally the humble oat which features in so much more than just porridge, including breads, puddings and even my version of Danish *romkugler* truffles, where it adds a lovely little crunch.

Almonds – along with most other Scandis, my family and I love almonds, whether whole, flaked, ground, toasted or in the form of marzipan and buttery almond pastes. These take starring roles in many cakes, buns and Danish pastries, and in *mazarin* (Scandi frangipane). Almonds are also the essential ingredient in *kransekake,* a chewy macaroon that is traditionally used to build decorated edible conical towers and horns of plenty to celebrate festive occasions.

Spices – I've said it before and I'll say it again: spices are for life, not just for Christmas! Cinnamon, cardamom, nutmeg, caraway, clove, allspice, star anise, ginger – they all play their parts in Scandinavian baking. Crisp oat bran flatbread tastes fantastic sprinkled with cardamom sugar, aniseed and fennel add an extra dimension to sweet Swedish *sirapslimpa* bread, melt-in-the-mouth cheese *sablé* biscuits are given a twist with caraway seeds and zesty lemon madeleines are enhanced by warming nutmeg.

Seasonal fruit – local fruit, picked and eaten in season, features heavily in Scandinavian cuisine, not least due to the well-established culture of foraging. Berries and summer fruit have a special place in my affections too, as my grandparents, *farmor* and *farfar* Johansen, owned a fruit farm on the west coast of Norway. I cherish my childhood memories of seemingly endless summer days in Norway picking ripe berries to eat, bake in cakes and puddings or preserve as jam. Inspired by these, you'll find dishes in here using crimson sour cherries, juicy strawberries, plump blueberries and redcurrants, crunchy apples, honey-sweet greengages and prickly gooseberries, as well as fragrant elderflowers and lemon verbena. But don't think that the Scandi love of local seasonal fruit has to limit you. There's fun to be had combining traditional and modern, seasonal and exotic, like the marriage of blueberries and raspberries with heavenly home-made passion-fruit-lime curd in my take on classic Danish layercake, or the combination of spiced *pepperkaker* biscuits with juicy limes in my decadent *Scandilicious* key lime pie…

On a practical note, I always bake with fresh yeast for precision and consistency, but know that there may be times when you can't get hold of any, so I have given fast action dried yeast measurements as an alternative. Do be aware that different brands of fast action dried yeast can be of differing strengths, so if you find that your chosen brand is too active or has too prominent a yeast flavour, feel free to reduce the yeast quantities to the level that is right for you. Similarly, I have included a range of rising and proving times for the yeasted doughs, as yeast grows at different rates depending on the warmth of the day and your kitchen – the warmer the air, the faster the dough will rise, so baking in summer will generally be a speedier process than in winter unless you keep your kitchen toasty warm! This applies to all yeasted doughs, although those containing rye or wholemeal flour, spices or milk and butter will be slower to rise (fibre, spices and fat tend to slow the process). Finally, unless I specify otherwise, I use whole milk and slightly salted butter in my baking as I enjoy their flavour; however, if you need to use different products for health or taste reasons, please do substitute as necessary.

Hopefully you are now inspired to pop on your apron, roll up your sleeves and bake up a storm, whether it's to try your hand at some traditional Scandi baking – from crusty breads and Danish pastries to spiced buns and marzipan delicacies – or to rustle up one of my modern takes on Nordic favourites, whichever takes your fancy.

Happy Scandi baking!

Sig x

Breads, rolls and flatbreads

Whenever people ask me what I miss

most about living in Scandinavia, good bread generally tops the list (followed by great seafood, summer berries, open sandwiches and beautiful design!) So it is no surprise to see plenty of tasty bread recipes here, along with suggestions of what to eat with your freshly baked loaf – sweet and savoury butters, *smørbrød* toppings and fruit-packed jams.

Bread is incredibly satisfying to make and only needs a handful of ingredients – flour, a raising agent (yeast, sourdough or baking soda), liquid (water, beer or milk) and a smidgeon of salt. With these and a little skill, love and patience, you can bake delicious bread that knocks the socks off the standard commercial loaf.

I love the tactile nature of bread baking: the way the ingredients come together in your hands to make the soft, squidgy dough; the stretch and elasticity that develops as you knead; and the pleasure of using your hands to shape the doughy mass in to neat buns, dimpled flatbreads, rustic loaves, beautiful plaits and intricate twists and swirls.

Once you've mastered the basic techniques, there are so many variations in content and form that you need never tire of your daily crust – spelt sourdough, chewy pumpernickel, chocolate soda bread, plaited milk loaf, fruity *müsli* bread, seeded *rundstykker* rolls, flavoured breadsticks, salty *kringler* pretzels, maple-iced Advent bread, sweet Swedish *sirapslimpa*… All the recipes here feature on a regular basis in my baking, and now I hope they will in yours too.

Müsli bread
Barley bread
Kefir spelt sourdough
Danish pumpernickel
Norwegian *grovbrød* —
  rustic brown bread
Plaited milk loaf
Vanilla bread
Swedish *sirapslimpa* bread
Maple-iced fruity
  Advent bread
Pinnebrød — barbecued bread
Chocolate soda bread
Breadsticks three ways
Easy spelt picnic buns
Sesame *rundstykker* rolls
Grove rundstykker rye and
  spelt poppy seed rolls
Saltkringler —
  large salted pretzels
Soft polar flatbread
Crunchy mixed seed and
  rosemary flatbread
Crisp oat bran flatbread with
  cardamom sugar

Flavoured butters
  Horseradish and lemon butter
  Anchovy and dill butter
  Caraway and coriander butter
  Cinnamon and vanilla butter

Jams
  Strawberry freezer jam
  Sour cherry jam
  Greengage and vanilla jam
  Gooseberry and elderflower jam

Open sandwich toppings
  Strawberries and granola
  Hot smoked trout with radish,
    lemon and horseradish
  Crab and asparagus
  Grilled cheese, mushroom
    and hazelnut

Müsli bread

We Scandinavians love our muesli, and in this recipe it brings a wholesome crunch to a great breakfast bread. Dried apricots, dates and sour cherries add an extra tang, but you can vary the flavours according to taste, using the base recipe as your starting point. This bread is best eaten fresh on the day of baking, and then makes delicious breakfast toast for a good few days afterwards. Do note that if you are going to be leaving the dough to ferment overnight in the fridge, you only need to use half the quantity of yeast specified below.

MAKES 1 LOAF

150g muesli
150ml double cream
450g refined spelt (or plain) flour
25g oat bran
25g unsweetened desiccated coconut
1 tsp fine sea salt
1 tsp cinnamon, plus more for sprinkling
10g fresh yeast or 5g fast action dried yeast
1 tsp caster sugar (if using fresh yeast)
2 tbsp maple syrup
1 tbsp date syrup
250-290ml water
4 soft dried apricots, chopped
4 medjool dates, chopped
small handful dried sour cherries
1 tsp honey, diluted in 1 tbsp boiling water
cinnamon for sprinkling
mixed flakes for sprinkling (try spelt, barley, oat and rye)

Leave the muesli to soak in the cream in a small bowl for 15 minutes or so. Sift the flour, oat bran, coconut, salt and cinnamon together in a large bowl, sprinkle in the dried yeast (if using) and stir through. If using fresh yeast, cream it with the teaspoon of sugar in a small bowl and once it is liquid (after about 30 seconds), add to the dry ingredients.

Make a well in the middle of the dry ingredients, add the cream-muesli mixture, the two syrups and 250ml of the water. Stir everything together, gradually adding more of the water if you think it needs it, until the mixture comes off the sides of the bowl and looks – for want of a better word – doughy. Place the dough in a lightly oiled plastic bag or cover the bowl with lightly oiled clingfilm. Leave to rise in a warm place for 40-60 minutes or so until it has doubled in size, or leave overnight in the fridge. Be aware that if you keep the dough in a lightly oiled plastic bag in the fridge overnight, the carbon dioxide gas from fermentation will expand the bag so make sure you leave plenty of space around it. Test that the dough is sufficiently risen by gently poking it with your little finger – the indentation should stay put.

Lightly oil a baking sheet. Knock the dough back (having let it return to room temperature for 30 minutes or so if you left it to prove overnight), mix in the dried fruit, then form the dough in to an oblong, slightly fat sausage, about 20cm long and 15cm wide. Gently place on the baking sheet, cover with lightly oiled clingfilm and leave to prove for 45 minutes or so in a warm place until doubled in size. Lightly poke with your finger to check – if the dough doesn't spring back, it's finished proving. Preheat the oven to 220°C/200°C fan/gas mark 7.

Glaze the loaf with the diluted honey and sprinkle with a pinch or two of cinnamon and the mixed flakes. Splash a little water in the bottom of the oven to create steam to help the loaf rise, then bake on the upper middle shelf, turning down the heat after the first 10 minutes to 190°C/170°C fan/gas mark 5. Bake for a further 30-40 minutes or until the bread has risen well, feels firm to the touch and sounds hollow when you tap it on the base.

Remove from the tin and leave to cool on a wire rack before slicing and eat just as it is, or with some cinnamon and vanilla butter (page 51).

Barley bread

This rustic wholemeal loaf with its fabulous malty flavour was inspired by my friend Fiona's husband Trevor, who introduced me to the idea of adding barley to bread. Scandinavians use a lot of byggryn *(barley) – I love it in stews, soups and salads, and the addition of cooked pearl barley here gives this loaf a lovely texture and flavour. The barleycorn flour contains wheat and barley flours along with malted barley flakes and linseeds, and I like to sprinkle linseed and sesame seeds on top, but you can use different seeds if you prefer. Do note that if you are going to be leaving the dough to ferment overnight in the fridge, you only need to use half the quantity of yeast specified below.*

MAKES 1 LOAF

500g barleycorn flour
15g fresh yeast or 7g fast action
  dried yeast
1 tsp caster sugar (if using fresh yeast)
350ml cold water

1 tbsp vegetable oil
1 tbsp treacle
1½ tsp salt
100g cooked pearl barley
mixed seeds for sprinkling

Sift the flour in to a large bowl, sprinkle in the dried yeast (if using) and stir through. If using fresh yeast, cream it with the teaspoon of sugar in a small bowl and once it is liquid (after about 30 seconds), add to the dry ingredients.

Make a well in the middle of the dry ingredients, add the water, oil, treacle, salt and barley, then stir everything together until the mixture comes off the sides of the bowl and looks – for want of a better word – doughy. Place the dough in a lightly oiled plastic bag or cover the bowl with lightly oiled clingfilm. Leave to rise in a warm place for 45-60 minutes or so until it has doubled in size, or leave overnight in the fridge. Be aware that if you keep the dough in a lightly oiled plastic bag in the fridge overnight, the carbon dioxide gas from fermentation will expand the bag so make sure you leave plenty of space around it. Test that the dough is sufficiently risen by gently poking it with your little finger – the indentation should stay put.

Lightly oil a 900g loaf tin. Knock the dough back (having let it return to room temperature for 30 minutes or so if you left it to prove overnight), shape in to an oblong loaf and gently place in the tin. Sprinkle with the seeds, cover with lightly oiled clingfilm and leave to prove for 45 minutes or so in a warm place until doubled in size. Lightly poke with your finger to check – if the dough doesn't spring back, it's finished proving. Preheat the oven to 220°C/200°C fan/gas mark 7.

Splash a little water in the bottom of the oven to create steam to help the loaf rise, then bake on the upper middle shelf, turning down the heat after the first 10 minutes to 190°C/170°C fan/gas mark 5. Bake for a further 30-40 minutes or until the bread has risen well, feels firm to the touch and sounds hollow when you tap it on the base.

Remove from the tin and leave to cool on a wire rack before slicing and eating with lots of butter. I find it hard resisting eating bread fresh from the oven, but if you have more willpower than me, you'll find that this keeps well for a few days and toasts well. Great with some brown cheese or Jarlsberg on top!

Kefir spelt sourdough

Making and maintaining a sourdough culture can be tricky, but then I came across the idea of making an easy sourdough starter using kefir milk, made from kefir grains. I love drinking kefir milk, and the various naturally occurring yeasts and probiotics which give the milk a tangy spritz make for a really active, lively starter, which is also great for making sourdough pancakes. This is not a speedy recipe as you will need to make the starter at least a day before you want to bake this bread, and the second proving can take up to a day too – but I think it is worth the wait!

MAKES 1 LOAF

Kefir starter
200g refined spelt
 (or plain) flour
200ml kefir milk

Dough
100g wholemeal spelt
 (or wheat) flour
200g refined spelt
 (or plain) flour, plus
 more for dusting
75ml milk
75ml water
1½ tsp fine sea salt

Make the sourdough starter by mixing the flour and kefir milk in a medium-sized bowl, stirring until it looks quite sticky. Cover with a clean tea towel and leave to grow at room temperature over the course of 24 hours. Check after 12 hours that it's bubbling and smelling fresh. Check again after another 12 hours, stir and then either use for your baking or leave for a further 12-24 hours if you wish. The longer you leave the starter the more time the yeast will have to multiply and the more complex and tangy the flavour will be.

On the day you want to bake the sourdough, stir the kefir starter and transfer it to a larger bowl. Add the dough ingredients and stir through until you have a smooth, pliable dough that comes off the sides of the bowl easily. If it's quite tough and dense, add a smidgeon more water and stir until you have the consistency you need to knead the dough. If it's too sticky, simply mix in a little more flour.

Using a dough scraper, keep lifting and kneading the dough for 30 seconds then place in a floured clean bowl. Cover with lightly oiled clingfilm or a teatowel and allow to double in size before knocking back and shaping in to a round ball. Place on a lightly oiled baking sheet and prove in a warm place one final time until it has doubled in size and the indentation left by a gentle prod with your finger doesn't spring back – depending on the temperature and the liveliness of the kefir this can take an hour or it could take all day so best to make this when you have some time on your hands.

Preheat the oven to 220°C/200°C fan/gas mark 7. Dust the loaf with a little flour. Splash a little water in the bottom of the oven to create steam to help the loaf rise, then bake on the upper middle shelf, turning the heat down after the first 10 minutes to 200°C/180°C fan/gas mark 6. Bake for a further 30-40 minutes or until the bread is golden brown and sounds hollow when you tap it on the base.

Remove from the tin and allow to cool on a wire rack before eating.

Danish pumpernickel

Rye bread has a centuries-long history in central Europe and you can find variations ranging from the traditional dark dense pumpernickel loaves so popular in Germany and Denmark, to the pale rye breads that travelled with the migrants across to America. Boiling the rye seems such a peculiar way of making bread; however, it converts the starch in to sugar, giving a sweeter taste and more complex flavour. I adore this bread topped with smoked salmon, crème fraîche, finely chopped red onion and capers, but it's equally good with herring, robustly flavoured charcuterie or just on its own with butter. Plus it improves with time, so try to resist the temptation to eat it all at once!

MAKES 1 LOAF

250g rye flour
250g strong white bread flour
50g rye flakes
1½ tsp fine sea salt
400ml boiling water
45g butter

45g treacle,
  plus 1 tsp for glazing
2 tsp caraway seeds
10g fresh yeast or
  5g fast action dried yeast
1 tsp caster sugar
  (if using fresh yeast)

Stir the flours, rye flakes, and salt together in a medium-sized bowl, then stir in the water with a wooden spoon until it forms a firm paste. Once it's cool enough to handle, pat down firmly with the palm of your hand to ensure that the water is completely absorbed by the rye flour. Leave to cool.

Melt the butter with the treacle and caraway seeds in a small saucepan. Pour this over the cooled flour paste and allow to cool slightly before adding the yeast. If using fresh yeast, cream it with the teaspoon of sugar in a small bowl first, then when it is liquid (after about 30 seconds) stir in to the flour-butter-treacle mix.

Knead for a couple of minutes. This is meant to be a dense dough so don't worry about working it for too long – just bring it together so that all the ingredients are distributed. The dough should be slightly sticky, so use a dough scraper to keep it moving and wet your hands with water to reduce sticking.

Cover with lightly oiled clingfilm and leave to prove in a warm place for 5 hours (or overnight) until the dough has risen – it won't puff up in the same way as other doughs and is meant to be rough, so don't fret if it looks lumpy and a bit sad.

Lightly oil a 900ml loaf tin. Knock back the dough for 30 seconds or so, then shape it in to a loaf and place in the tin. Cover with the oiled clingfilm again and allow to prove in a warm place for a further hour or until the dough doesn't spring back when lightly poked with your finger.

Preheat the oven to 220°C/200°C fan/gas mark 7. Put the teaspoon of treacle in a small bowl and stir in a tablespoon of boiling water. Lightly brush the dough with the treacle glaze, giving it one or two coats, for a dark crust. Splash a little water in the bottom of the oven to create steam to help the loaf rise, then bake on the upper middle shelf, turning the heat down after the first 10 minutes to 200°C/180°C fan/gas mark 6. Bake for a further 30-40 minutes or until the bread is dark brown and sounds hollow when you tap it on the base.

Remove the loaf from its tin and allow to cool on a wire rack. This bread keeps well for up to a week but doesn't freeze well (it goes dry and crumbly), so you have the perfect excuse to eat it while it's fresh!

VARIATION

If you fancy a wholegrain rye bread, soak 50g whole rye grains in water overnight and add to the dough with the rye flakes.

Norwegian *grovbrød* – rustic brown bread

One of the many things I miss most about living in Scandinavia is the bread. My first port of call whenever I return is always a bakery, to buy a few loaves of good Norwegian grovbrød. *I've even been known to pack bread in my suitcase to take home! I think classic wholemeal* grovbrød *really separates the wheat from the chaff, quite literally, as it's packed full of fibre. When it's fresh there is nothing better with a couple of slices of cheese or just eaten plain with good butter. Do note that if you are going to be leaving the dough to ferment overnight in the fridge, you only need to use half the quantity of yeast specifed below.*

MAKES 1 LOAF

200g refined spelt (or plain) flour
100g wholemeal spelt (or wheat) flour
100g rye flour
50g oat bran
50g wheatgerm
10g fresh yeast or 5g fast action dried yeast
1 tsp caster sugar (if using fresh yeast)
2 tsp treacle
1 tbsp vegetable oil
1½ tsp fine sea salt
375-390ml water

Sift all the dry ingredients together in a large bowl, sprinkle in the dried yeast (if using) and stir through. If using fresh yeast, cream it with the teaspoon of sugar in a small bowl and once it is liquid (after about 30 seconds), add to the dry ingredients.

Make a well in the middle of the dry ingredients, add the treacle, oil, salt and 375ml of the water. Stir everything together, gradually adding more of the water if you think it needs it, until the mixture comes off the sides of the bowl and looks – for want of a better word – doughy. Place the dough in a lightly oiled plastic bag or cover the bowl with lightly oiled clingfilm. Leave to rise in a warm place for 45-60 minutes or so until it has doubled in size, or leave overnight in the fridge. Be aware that if you keep the dough in a lightly oiled plastic bag in the fridge overnight, the carbon dioxide gas from fermentation will expand the bag so make sure you leave plenty of space around it. Test that the dough is sufficiently risen by gently poking it with your little finger – the indentation should stay put.

Lightly oil a 900g loaf tin. Knock the dough back (having let it return to room temperature for 30 minutes or so if you left it to prove overnight), shape the dough in to an oblong loaf and gently place in the tin. Cover with lightly oiled clingfilm and leave to prove for 45 minutes or so in a warm place until doubled in size. Lightly poke with your finger to check – if the dough doesn't spring back, it's finished proving. Preheat the oven to 220°C/200°C fan/gas mark 7.

Splash a little water in the bottom of the oven to create steam to help the loaf rise, then bake on the upper middle shelf, turning down the heat after the first 10 minutes to 190°C/170°C fan/gas mark 5. Bake for a further 30-40 minutes or until the bread has risen well, feels firm to the touch and sounds hollow when you tap it on the base.

Remove from the tin and leave to cool on a wire rack before slicing and eating with lots of butter. Freeze what you haven't used a day after baking, as this bread goes dry quite quickly.

Plaited milk loaf

There's nothing quite as delightful as a rich milk bread with its soft white crumb and shiny golden crust, and they make the most beautiful plaited loaves. This bread looks wonderfully festive and is a doddle to make. It's delicious eaten fresh on the day of baking and, if there's any left after that, makes great toast and French toast. Do note that if you are going to be leaving the dough to ferment overnight in the fridge, you only need to use half the quantity of yeast specified below.

MAKES 1 PLAIT

250ml whole milk
50g butter
500g refined spelt flour
 (or 250g plain flour
 and 250g strong flour)
50g caster sugar,
 plus 1 tsp (if using
 fresh yeast)
2 tsp fine sea salt
25g fresh yeast or 12g
 fast action dried yeast
1 medium egg, beaten,
 plus more to glaze
 (optional)

Scald the milk by heating it in a small pan with the butter until it is almost boiling and then allow it to cool while you assemble the other ingredients. Scalding the milk like this makes the finished bread softer.

Sift the flour(s), sugar and salt together in to a large bowl, sprinkle in the dried yeast (if using) and stir through. If using fresh yeast, cream it with a teaspoon of sugar in a small bowl and once it is liquid (after about 30 seconds), add to the dry ingredients.

Make a well in the middle of the dry ingredients. Pour in the beaten egg and then the milk-butter mixture, which should be warm rather than hot to the touch, as otherwise you risk killing the yeast. Stir everything together until the mixture comes off the sides of the bowl and looks – for want of a better word – doughy.

Place the dough in a lightly oiled plastic bag or cover the bowl with lightly oiled clingfilm. Leave to rise in a warm place for 45-60 minutes or so until it has doubled in size, or leave overnight in the fridge. Be aware that if you keep the dough in a lightly oiled plastic bag in the fridge overnight, the carbon dioxide gas from fermentation will expand the bag so make sure you leave plenty of space around it. You can test the dough to see whether it has risen sufficiently by gently poking it with your little finger – the indentation should stay put.

Take the dough out of the fridge and let it return to room temperature for 30 minutes or so if you left it to prove overnight. Knock back the dough, then divide in three equal portions – the easiest way is to weigh it and divide the total by 3 to give the weight of each piece. Roll each third in to a long sausage about 3-5cm in diameter. Lie the three sausages side by side so that you are looking down their lengths, and then press the farthest tips together, creating a tripod shape, so they don't unravel while you plait them. Once you've plaited the full lenth of the sausages, press the ends together and brush with water to seal the loaf. You can then either leave the end as it is or tuck it lightly under the plait to round the loaf off. Place on a lightly oiled baking sheet, cover and leave to prove in a warm place for an hour or so until the dough no longer springs back when pressed with your little finger.

Preheat the oven to 220°C/200°C fan/gas mark 7. Brush the plait with beaten egg (or with water if you don't want a gloss on the crust). Splash a little water in the bottom of the oven to create steam to help the loaf rise, then bake on the upper middle shelf, turning the heat down after the first 10 minutes to 200°C/180°C fan/gas mark 6. Bake for a further 35-40 minutes or so until the plait looks golden brown and sounds hollow when you tap it on the base.

Allow to cool on a wire rack, impatiently awaiting that first delicious slice…

Vanilla bread

This vanilla-scented variation on the traditional milk loaf is one of my favourite breakfast breads. I can highly recommend eating this with a dab of delicious butter and a couple of spoonfuls of strawberry freezer jam (see recipe on page 53). It also makes great toast and French toast for a good few days after baking. Do note that if you are going to be leaving the dough to ferment overnight in the fridge, you only need to use half the quantity of yeast specified below.

MAKES 1 LOAF

½ vanilla pod, split
250ml whole milk, plus more to glaze (optional)
50g butter
1 tbsp vanilla extract
500g refined spelt (or plain) flour
50g caster sugar, plus 1 tsp (if using fresh yeast)
1 tsp salt
25g fresh yeast or 12g fast action dried yeast
1 medium egg, beaten

Scrape the seeds out of the vanilla pod and place in a small saucepan with the milk, butter and vanilla extract. Heat the milk mixture in a small pan until almost boiling and then allow to cool while you assemble the other ingredients. Scalding the milk like this makes the finished bread softer.

Sift the flour, sugar and salt together in to a large bowl, sprinkle in the dried yeast (if using) and stir through. If using fresh yeast, cream it with a teaspoon of sugar in a small bowl and once it is liquid (after about 30 seconds), add to the dry ingredients.

Make a well in the middle of the dry ingredients. Pour in the beaten egg and then the vanilla milk-butter mixture, which should be warm rather than hot to the touch, as otherwise you risk killing the yeast. Stir everything together until the mixture comes off the sides of the bowl and looks – for want of a better word – doughy.

Place the dough in a lightly oiled plastic bag or cover the bowl with lightly oiled clingfilm. Leave to rise in a warm place for 45-60 minutes or so until it has doubled in size, or leave overnight in the fridge. Be aware that if you keep the dough in a lightly oiled plastic bag in the fridge overnight, the carbon dioxide gas from fermentation will expand the bag so make sure you leave plenty of space around it. You can test the dough to see whether it has risen sufficiently by gently poking it with your little finger – the indentation should stay put.

Remove the dough from the fridge and leave to return to room temperature for 30 minutes or so if you left it to prove overnight. Lightly oil a 900g loaf tin. Knock back the dough, then shape in an oblong loaf shape and place gently in the tin. Cover and leave to prove in a warm place for an hour or so until the dough no longer springs back when pressed with your little finger.

Preheat the oven to 220°C/200°C fan/gas mark 7. Brush the dough with water or milk for a softer crust. Splash a little water in the bottom of the oven to create steam to help the loaf rise, then bake on the upper middle shelf, turning the heat down after the first 10 minutes to 200°C/180°C fan/gas mark 6. Bake for a further 35-40 minutes or so until the bread looks golden brown and sounds hollow when you tap it on the base.

Remove the tin and allow to cool on a wire rack before eating.

VARIATION

You can bake this dough as 16-20 buns instead of one loaf if you prefer. After the first proving, simply follow the method for easy spelt picnic buns on page 36.

Swedish *sirapslimpa* bread

Ex-pat Swedish friends tell me how much they miss their beloved limpa *or rustic wholemeal loaf.*
Sirapslimpa is a variation made and glazed with syrup, and this version flavoured with treacle, aniseed,
fennel and tangy orange zest is now a firm favourite in my household. Filmjölk, *a cultured, soured milk,*
is traditionally used in making this bread but it can be hard to find outside Scandinavia. I've used
buttermilk instead to give that extra soft crumb and slight tang, but if you have plain, unsweetened
pouring yoghurt or something similar then do give that a go (alternatively add 1½ teaspoons of lemon
juice or white wine/cider vinegar to 200ml whole milk to sour it). The bread has a faint orange colour
and tastes wonderful on its own or with butter and orange marmalade. Like pumpernickel it's also
excellent with cheese and other smørgåsbord *toppings.*

MAKES 1 LOAF

200g rye flour
200ml boiling water
40g butter
40g treacle, plus 1 tsp for glazing
1 tsp each of aniseed and fennel seeds
finely grated zest of ½ unwaxed orange
350g strong white bread flour
1½ tsp fine sea salt
200ml buttermilk
10g fresh yeast or 5g fast action dried yeast
1 tsp caster sugar (if using fresh yeast)

Put the rye flour in a medium bowl and pour the water over it. Stir until the flour is
thoroughly soaked and looks like a dense paste. Leave to cool while you melt the butter
with the treacle, aniseed and fennel seeds and the orange zest. Pour this mixture over the
rye paste. Add the strong white bread flour, salt, buttermilk and dried yeast (if using).
If using fresh yeast, cream it with the teaspoon of sugar in a small bowl and once it is
liquid (after about 30 seconds), add to the other ingredients. By this time, you will have
what looks like chaos in a bowl.

Using your hands squelch everything together. It will feel sticky and messy but that's
the fun of making *limpa*! Keep mixing with your hands until the dough starts coming
together in to a ball of sorts. Lightly dust the kitchen surface with some flour and place
the *limpa* dough on this. If your hands are very sticky use a little flour to clean them of
excess dough and give them a quick rinse – if you have sticky dough on your hands while
you're kneading you're creating unnecessary hard work for yourself and slowing down
the kneading process. Use a dough scraper to push and knead the dough as much as possible.
It won't be the lightest of doughs to manipulate but keep persisting and it will start to
become elastic and smooth-ish within about 5-8 minutes. Pop the dough in to a lightly
oiled plastic bag and leave to prove in the refrigerator overnight. Make sure you leave

plenty of space around the dough as the carbon dioxide gas from fermentation will expand the bag.

The next day remove the dough from the fridge, keeping the oiled plastic bag, and allow to come to room temperature for half an hour or so before you knock back the dough and shape it in to a smooth, round loaf. It should look a little like a half football so the more you dome it the better. Place this on a lightly oiled baking tray and cover with the lightly oiled plastic bag (you can tear this slightly if necessary so it fits more snugly over the bread). Leave to prove in a warm place for 1 hour or until the dough has risen and when prodded leaves a small imprint of your finger.

Preheat the oven to 220°C/200°C fan/gas mark 7. Dilute the treacle with a tablespoon of boiling water in a small bowl. Use a pastry brush to glaze the surface of the proved *limpa* dough so it has a nice coating of treacle – this will give a lovely colour and slightly sweet crust.

Splash some water on the bottom of your oven to create steam for the bread to really spring up. Bake the bread on the middle shelf for 10 minutes, then reduce the heat to 200°C/180°C fan/gas mark 6 and bake a further 30 minutes or until the bread looks dark brown and sounds hollow when tapped on the base.

Allow to cool on a wire rack before slicing and eating greedily!

VARIATIONS

You could add a generous handful of soaked raisins to the dough for a sweeter bread, or some chopped walnuts, or indeed both.

It's also common in Sweden to add candied orange or lemon peel for a little extra citrus sweetness.

Other seeds such as caraway, cumin, coriander or linseeds would be delicious in this bread too.

Maple-iced fruity Advent bread

Advent in the Johansen household is all about baking, and great bread is a must. This is a delicious sweet loaf dotted with boozy fruit – I use a mix of apricots, cranberries, sour cherries, raisins, prunes, chopped dates and figs. I spike the fruit with Manzanilla sherry due to my particular fondess for its nutty, slightly saline flavour, but by all means use your favourite tipple – brandy, rum and calvados all work really well. The maple icing is optional but adds a little sweet decadence.

MAKES 1 LOAF

250ml whole milk
75g butter
300g refined spelt (or plain) flour
125g wholemeal spelt (or wheat) flour
70g caster sugar, plus 1 tsp (if using fresh yeast)
1 tsp ground cardamom
½ tsp salt
20g fresh yeast or 10g fast action dried yeast
1 medium egg, beaten
50ml Manzanilla sherry
150g mixed dried fruit, chopped
1 medium egg, beaten, to glaze

To finish
150g icing sugar
1 tsp cinnamon
3-4 tbsp maple syrup

Scald the milk by heating it in a small pan with the butter until it is almost boiling and then leave to cool while you assemble the other ingredients. Scalding the milk makes the finished bread softer.

Sift all the dry ingredients together in a large bowl, sprinkle in the dried yeast (if using) and stir through. If using fresh yeast, cream it with a teaspoon of sugar in a small bowl and once it is liquid (after about 30 seconds), add to the dry ingredients.

Make a well in the middle of the dry ingredients. Add the beaten egg and then the milk-butter mixture, which should be warm rather than hot to the touch, as otherwise you risk killing the yeast. Stir everything together until the mixture comes off the sides of the bowl and looks – for want of a better word – doughy. Place the dough in a lightly oiled plastic bag or cover the bowl with lightly oiled clingfilm. Leave to rise in a warm place for 45-60 minutes or so until doubled in size and springy to the touch.

While the dough is rising, pour the sherry over the dried fruit in a medium-sized bowl, topping up with water if necessary to ensure that the fruit is fully covered. Leave to soak for 30 minutes before draining off any excess liquid (don't throw this away, as it's great for using in fruit salads or for adding to sweet sauces).

Knock the dough back for 10 seconds or so, then add the fruit and mix through by hand so it is evenly distributed. Shape in to a rough loaf shape about 20cm long – the end result is meant to look flat and rustic so don't worry about shaping it in to anything fancy. Cover the dough again and leave to prove in a warm place for a further 45-60 minutes of so, until the dough no longer springs back: you can test it by gently poking it with your little finger – the indentation should stay put.

Preheat the oven to 200°C/180°C fan/gas mark 6. Glaze the risen dough with beaten egg and bake on the middle shelf of the oven for 40-45 minutes until the bread sounds hollow when tapped on the base. Allow to cool completely on a wire rack.

When the bread is cool, mix the icing sugar, cinnamon and maple syrup together. It should form a sticky icing, not too runny. Drizzle the icing all over the bread and allow to set completely. If you have any left over (and you can resist the urge to lick the bowl clean!), you could drizzle a second layer on later, or keep it for icing gingerbread or other cakes.

Pinnebrød – barbecued bread

Barbecued bread is a really popular summertime tradition in Scandinavia, and this recipe is adapted from one in Morten Schakenda's fantastic Norwegian baking book for children. As kids, we used to make the dough in class, then pack it in our rucksacks to take on field trips to the forest near our school in Oslo. We wrapped the dough around green twigs and barbecued it over the campfire embers. I've suggested that you use skewers instead of twigs to avoid getting any bark in your bread (although it never did me any harm), and if you haven't got a campfire handy, simply use the barbecue. Do remember to wait until the embers turn grey before you cook your dough, as open flames will scorch the crust and make it taste acrid. Cooking bread like this is a great activity with kids – with close supervision of course!

MAKES 10 SKEWERS

290ml whole milk
50g butter
1 tbsp treacle
400g refined spelt
 (or plain) flour
100g wholemeal spelt
 (or rye) flour
1½ tsp sea salt
15g fresh yeast or 7g
 fast action dried yeast
1 tsp caster sugar
 (if using fresh yeast)
1 medium egg

If using wooden skewers, soak them in cold water for 30 minutes before using to prevent them from burning. Heat 250ml of the milk, the butter and the treacle in a small saucepan to just below boiling point, remove from the heat and allow to cool to blood temperature (it needs to be below 50°C before adding to the yeast, as otherwise you risk killing it).

Sift the flours, salt and dried yeast (if using) in a large mixing bowl and mix thoroughly so the salt and yeast are evenly distributed. If using fresh yeast, cream it with a teaspoon of sugar in a small bowl and once it is liquid (after about 30 seconds), add to the dry ingredients.

Make a hollow in the dry ingredients and use a wooden spoon to stir in the lukewarm milk-butter-treacle mixture in two stages, then stir in the egg. When the mixture begins to come together, scrape the dough off the spoon and continue to mix with your hands, adding as much of the rest of the milk as is needed to form a slightly sticky (but definitely not wet) dough. Turn the dough out on a floured board or surface and knead for 5 minutes (ideally using a plastic or metal dough scraper) until it springs back when you press it lightly with your thumb.

IF YOU'RE BARBECUING AT HOME: Transfer the dough back to the mixing bowl, cover with lightly oiled clingfilm and leave to rise somewhere warm for 45-60 minutes or until it has doubled in size.

IF YOU'RE OFF HIKING: Pop in a lightly oiled, large plastic bag, tie a knot and put in your rucksack. Take the dough out after you've been walking or hiking for a few hours, by which time it should have doubled in size.

Divide the dough in 10 pieces and roll in to rough sausage shapes, each about 20cm long. Starting about one-third of the way along each skewer, twine the dough around it, leaving a slight separation between each twirl to allow the bread to cook through properly. Press the end of the dough on to the tip of the skewer, to secure it. Hold the skewers above the embers of the fire or place on the barbecue and cook until the crust is light brown and feels firm to the touch. Remember to keep a teatowel to hand if you are using metal skewers so that you don't burn your fingers.

This bread doesn't really keep, which is a great excuse to eat it all up while it's warm – just as it is or dipped in melted butter (see page 50 for flavoured butters). You could also make it sweet, a sort of barbecued doughnut, by rolling the bread in a spiced sugar mixture or maple syrup while it is still warm from the fire.

Chocolate soda bread

Soda bread is the perfect beginner's bread as it requires no kneading. Don't be afraid to thrash the dough about in the bowl with a large spoon, but make sure to get the loaf baking as soon as possible, as the bicarbonate of soda starts working as soon as it is mixed with liquid. This rich brown bread is great on its own with a slab of good butter or topped with cheese, smoked salmon, ham, marmalade, chocolate hazelnut spread... pretty much anything really! If you can't get hold of buttermilk, just add 5 teaspoons of lemon juice or white wine/cider vinegar to 750ml whole milk to sour it.

MAKES 1 LOAF

200g rye flour	2 tbsp cocoa powder
200g refined spelt (or plain) flour	1 tsp bicarbonate of soda
100g porridge oats	½ tsp salt
100g wheatgerm	3 medium eggs, beaten
100g oat bran	750ml buttermilk
75g brown sugar	1 tbsp treacle (or molasses)

Preheat the oven to 220°C/200°C fan/gas mark 7. Lightly oil one large or two small loaf tins.

Place all the dry ingredients in a large mixing bowl and stir with a spoon to distribute the soda. Make a well in the middle of the dry ingredients and add the liquid ingredients. Mix thoroughly – it will be quite a sticky wet dough.

Pour the mixture in to the oiled loaf tin(s) and bake for 15 minutes, then turn the temperature down to 180°C/160°C fan/gas mark 4. Bake for a further 30-40 minutes or until the bread is golden brown, feels firm to the touch and sounds hollow when you tap it on the base.

Allow to rest in the tin for 10 minutes before removing to a wire rack to cool (although I can never resist eating the first slice covered in a puddle of melting butter while the bread is still hot from the oven).

Breadsticks three ways

Breadsticks are very versatile – perfect to nibble on at a picnic lunch, as a healthy(ish) snack or to serve with drinks and dips at a party. I love the smoked sea salt ones and the salted lavender ones are particularly good for dipping in creamy goat's cheese. You can ring the changes with the herbs and spices in the third topping option by substituting finely crushed black or white pepper, crushed cardamom seeds, dill, fennel seeds or aniseeds for the allspice.

MAKES ABOUT 20

500g strong white flour
2 tsp salt
25g fresh yeast or
  12g fast action
  dried yeast
1 tsp caster sugar
  (if using fresh yeast)
1 tbsp grapeseed,
  sunflower or
  vegetable oil
300-350ml water
25g butter, melted

Topping 1
2 tbsp smoked sea salt

Topping 2
2 tbsp sea salt
1 tbsp crushed lavender

Topping 3
2 tbsp sea salt
1 tsp allspice

Line 1 large or 2 medium baking trays with baking parchment. Sift the flour and salt in a large bowl, sprinkle in the dried yeast (if using) and stir through. If using fresh yeast, cream it with a teaspoon of sugar in a small bowl and once it is liquid (after about 30 seconds), add to the dry ingredients.

Make a well in the middle of the dry ingredients, add the oil and water and stir everything together until the mixture comes off the sides of the bowl and looks – for want of a better word – doughy. Take the dough out and knead it until it starts stretching – it should look smooth and feel springy. You really want to stretch the gluten strands in this breadstick dough so use those upper arms and think of the toning workout you're getting! Once the dough looks smooth and springs back when you poke it, place in a lightly oiled plastic bag or cover the bowl with lightly oiled clingfilm. Leave it to rise in a warm place for 45-60 minutes.

Remove the dough from the bag or bowl and knock back by punching the air out of the dough for 30 seconds. Weigh the dough if you want to be precise and divide the total weight by 20 in order to work out how much dough to use for each breadstick. Otherwise simply divide the dough in to 20 roughly equal pieces.

Roll each bit of dough in to a finger-width breadstick, place it on the prepared baking sheet and brush with melted butter before sprinkling with the topping of your choice. Cover and leave to prove in a warm place for 15-30 minutes or so until doubled in size. Lightly poke with your finger to check – if the dough doesn't spring back, it's finished proving.

Preheat the oven to 200°C/180°C fan/gas mark 6. Splash a little water in the bottom of the oven to create steam which will help the bread-sticks puff up when baking. Bake on the upper-middle shelf of the oven for 8-10 minutes or until the breadsticks look golden and sound hollow when you tap them on the base. If you're using two trays, swap them halfway through cooking so that the breadsticks bake evenly.

Allow to cool on wire racks. Serve upright in glasses or cups.

Easy spelt picnic buns

Perfect for lunch boxes, picnics or when you need something to get you through the afternoon. I bake these in muffin tins as it removes the need to form bun shapes – the dough naturally domes upwards as it bakes – so making these is as easy as 1-2-3! I like to sprinkle the tops with a mix of linseed, sunflower, pumpkin, sesame, hemp and poppy seeds, but feel free to use a different mix or to stick to just one type of seed if you prefer.

MAKES 12

290ml whole milk
45g butter
2 tbsp treacle or clear honey
200g refined spelt (or plain) flour
140g wholemeal spelt (or wheat) flour
1 tsp salt
15g fresh yeast or 7g fast action dried yeast
1 tsp caster sugar (if using fresh yeast)
1 medium egg, beaten
handful mixed seeds
handful oat or spelt flakes (optional)

Heat 250ml of the milk, butter and treacle or honey in a small saucepan to just below boiling point, remove from the heat and allow to cool to blood temperature (it needs to be below 50°C before adding to the yeast, as otherwise you risk killing it).

Sift the flours, salt and dried yeast (if using) in a large mixing bowl and mix thoroughly so the salt and yeast are evenly distributed. If using fresh yeast, cream it with a teaspoon of sugar in a small bowl and once it is liquid (after about 30 seconds), add to the dry ingredients.

Make a hollow in the dry ingredients and use a wooden spoon to stir in the lukewarm milk-butter-treacle mixture in two stages. When the mixture begins to come together, scrape the dough off the spoon and continue to mix with your hands, adding as much of the rest of the milk as is needed to form a slightly sticky (but definitely not wet) dough. Turn the dough out on a floured board or surface and knead for 5 minutes (ideally using a plastic or metal dough scraper) until it springs back when you press it lightly with your thumb.

Turn the dough out on a floured board or surface and knead for 5 minutes (ideally using a plastic or metal dough scraper) until it springs back when you press it lightly with your thumb. Transfer the dough to the mixing bowl again, cover with lightly oiled clingfilm and leave to rise in a warm place for 45-60 minutes or until it has doubled in size. While it is proving, lightly oil a 12-hole medium-sized muffin tin.

Knock the risen dough back by giving it a couple of punches. Knead gently on a floured surface for a couple of minutes then divide in to 12 pieces (either by weighing or judging by eye). Put the dough pieces in the muffin tray, cover with lightly oiled clingfilm and leave to prove in a warm place for a further 20-30 minutes or until they have doubled in size (it's worth checking the dough regularly if you're using spelt flour, as I find it has a tendency to prove quickly).

Preheat the oven to 220°C/200°C fan/gas mark 7. Brush the top of the buns with beaten egg and sprinkle with a handful of mixed seeds and oat or spelt flakes (if using).

Splash a little water in the bottom of the oven to create steam to help the buns to rise. Bake on the upper middle shelf of the oven for 5 minutes before turning the heat down to 190°C/170°C fan/gas mark 5 and baking for a further 10-15 minutes until the buns sound hollow if tapped on the base.

Leave to cool in the tin for 10 minutes, then turn out on a wire rack to cool.

These buns taste best on the day they're baked, so if you won't be getting through them all, why not freeze some for another day? Just reheat wrapped in foil at 150°C/130°C fan/gas mark 2 for 10 minutes, then remove the foil and bake at 190°C/170°C fan/gas mark 5 for 5 minutes for freshly baked buns all over again.

Sesame *rundstykker* rolls

Rundstykker *(literally 'round pieces') are a much-loved baking tradition in Scandinavia.*
My Norwegian grandmother made great little rundstykker *like these, and they're a real breakfast*
hit with children and adults alike. I find it's worth making large batches (double the quantities below)
and freezing any that haven't been eaten within a few days, as they reheat really well – just refresh at
150°C/130°C fan/gas mark 2 for 5-10 minutes. I tend to bake rundstykker *quite close together in*
a rectangular baking tin so that they join up as they prove and bake – they can then be pulled apart
when sharing with family and friends. Of course you can make them smaller and/or space them out on
a large baking sheet if you'd prefer to keep them separate. Do note that if you leave the dough to ferment
overnight in the fridge you only need to use half the quantity of yeast specified below.

MAKES 12 MEDIUM-SIZED ROLLS

250ml whole milk
50g butter
400g refined spelt (or plain) flour
100g wholemeal spelt (or wheat) flour
2 tsp fine sea salt
15g fresh yeast or 7g fast action dried yeast
1 tsp caster sugar (if using fresh yeast)
1 medium egg, beaten (or 2-3 tbsp milk) to glaze
sesame seeds for sprinkling

Scald the milk by heating it in a small pan with the butter until it is almost boiling and then allow it to cool while you assemble the other ingredients. Scalding the milk makes the finished rolls softer.

Sift the flours and salt together in a large bowl, sprinkle in the dried yeast (if using) and stir through. If using fresh yeast, cream it with a teaspoon of sugar in a small bowl and once it is liquid (after about 30 seconds), add to the dry ingredients.

Make a well in the middle of the dry ingredients and add the scalded milk, which should be warm rather than hot to the touch, as otherwise you risk killing the yeast. Stir everything together until the mixture comes off the sides of the bowl and looks – for want of a better word – doughy.

Cover the dough with lightly oiled clingfilm and leave it to rise in a warm place for 45-60 minutes until it has doubled in size, or put in a lightly oiled plastic bag and leave overnight in the fridge. Be aware that the carbon dioxide gas from fermentation will expand the bag so make sure you leave plenty of space around the dough. You can test the dough to see whether it has risen sufficiently by gently poking it with your little finger – the indentation should stay put.

If you proved the dough in the fridge overnight, let it return to room temperature for 30 minutes or so. Preheat the oven to 220°C/200°C fan/gas mark 7 and lightly oil two 20cm x 30cm rectangular baking tins.

Knock the risen dough back by giving it a couple of punches. Knead gently on a floured surface for a couple of minutes then divide in to 12 roughly equal-sized portions (either judging by eye or by weighing the dough, whichever you prefer). Shape the pieces in to rolls and place in the baking tins. Cover with lightly oiled clingfilm and leave to prove in a warm place for 15-30 minutes or so, until the rolls don't spring back any more when you poke them. Brush with beaten egg (or milk) and top with a generous scattering of sesame seeds.

Splash a little water in the bottom of the oven to create steam to help the rolls to rise. Bake on the middle shelf for 10 minutes, then reduce the heat to 190°C/170°C fan/gas mark 5 and bake for a further 5-10 minutes or until the rolls are golden brown and sound hollow when you tap them on the base.

Remove from the oven and allow to cool on a wire rack.

Grove rundstykker rye and spelt poppy seed rolls

The traditional Scandinavian breakfast smörgåsbord *is a thing of beauty, with its amazing array of fresh breads, cheeses, hams, fish, jams, yoghurt, fruit and pastries… I particularly love the freshly baked* grove rundstykker *or wholemeal bread rolls, and these rye and spelt rolls, topped with poppy seeds, make a delicious contrast to the lighter sesame* rundstykker *(see page 39). Great on their own, fresh from the oven, with a generous wodge of butter melting in the middle or sandwiched around a thick slice of good cheese, these* rundstykker *also freeze well, so why not make a double batch so that you have some to pop in the freezer once cooled. Then just refresh them in a 150°C/130°C fan/gas mark 2 oven for 5-10 minutes for hot crusty rolls on lazy weekend mornings. Do note that if you leave the dough to ferment overnight in the fridge you only need to use half the quantity of yeast specified below.*

MAKES 20 MEDIUM-SIZED ROLLS

150ml whole milk
350g refined spelt (or plain) flour
150g rye flour
2 tsp salt
25g fresh yeast or 12g fast action dried yeast
1 tsp caster sugar (if using fresh yeast)
200ml soured cream
1 tbsp clear honey
poppy seeds for sprinkling

Scald the milk by heating it in a small pan until it is almost boiling and then allow it to cool while you assemble the other ingredients. Scalding the milk makes the finished rolls softer.

Sift all the dry ingredients together in to a large bowl, sprinkle the dried yeast in and stir through. If using fresh yeast, cream it with a teaspoon of sugar in a small bowl and once it is liquid (after about 30 seconds), add to the dry ingredients.

Make a well in the middle of the dry ingredients, add the scalded milk, which should be warm rather than hot to the touch, as otherwise you risk killing the yeast. Add the soured cream and honey, then stir everything together until the mixture comes off the sides of the bowl and looks – for want of a better word – doughy.

Cover the dough with lightly oiled clingfilm and leave it to rise in a warm place for 45-60 minutes until it has doubled in size, or put in a lightly oiled plastic bag and leave overnight in the fridge. Be aware that the carbon dioxide gas from fermentation will expand the bag so make sure you leave plenty of space around the dough. You can test the dough to see whether it has risen sufficiently by gently poking it with your little finger – the indentation should stay put.

If you proved the dough in the fridge overnight, allow to return to room temperature for 30 minutes or so. Preheat the oven to 220°C/200°C fan/gas mark 7.

Knock the risen dough back by giving it a couple of punches. Knead gently on a floured surface for a couple of minutes then divide in to 20 roughly equal-sized portions and shape each one in to a ball. Cover with lightly oiled clingfilm and leave to prove in a warm place for 15-30 minutes or so, until the rolls don't spring back any more when you poke them. Brush with water and sprinkle a good layer of poppy seeds on top.

Splash a little water in the bottom of the oven to create steam to help the rolls to rise. Bake on the upper middle shelf of the oven for 10 minutes, then reduce the heat to 190°C/170°C fan/gas mark 5 and bake for a further 5-10 minutes or until the rolls are pale brown and sound hollow when you tap them on the base.

Remove the *rundstykker* from the oven and allow to cool on a wire rack before eating, if you have more willpower than me…

Saltkringler – large salted pretzels

*Many people associate the pretzel with Germany but it can be found all across
Scandinavia too, and in Denmark a golden pretzel-shaped sign dangling above the
door has long been the symbol for a bakery. Salt pretzels, or saltkringler in Danish,
are wonderful with a glass of cold beer or as a snack when you're out on a walk
in the mountains or woods. The secret behind the distinctive shiny brown finish
is the bicarbonate of soda in the water the pretzels are boiled in. The addition of
crunchy or flaked sea salt (rather than fine salt) really adds texture and flavour so
don't be afraid of generously sprinkling it on before baking.*

500g strong white flour
1 tsp salt
15g fresh yeast or 7g fast action dried yeast
1 tsp caster sugar (if using fresh yeast)
30ml clear honey
1 tbsp oil
3 tbsp bicarbonate of soda (for boiling)
small handful crunchy or flaky sea salt
sesame and poppy seeds (optional)

Sift the flour and salt together in to a large bowl, sprinkle in the dried yeast (if using) and stir through. If using fresh yeast, cream it with a teaspoon of sugar in a small bowl and once it is liquid (after about 30 seconds) add to the dry ingredients.

Make a well in the middle of the dry ingredients, and add the honey and oil. Stir everything together until the mixture comes off the sides of the bowl and looks – for want of a better word – doughy. Really knead the dough for a good 10 minutes: it should be quite tough so it holds its shape while boiling and baking.

Cover with lightly oiled clingfilm and leave to prove in a warm place for 45-60 minutes or until the dough has doubled in size. Knock back and allow to prove in a warm place for a further 30-45 minutes or so until there is no more spring back when you poke the dough gently with your little finger.

Preheat the oven to 225°C/205°C fan/gas mark 7-8 and lightly oil one large or two medium baking sheets. Divide the dough in to 10 even-sized balls. Keep the unworked doughballs covered with lightly oiled clingfilm or a teatowel as you shape one piece at a time in to a long sausage, about 1cm in diameter, then twist it in to the traditional pretzel shape. Dab the ends with water and press them to the main part of the pretzel to stick them in place. Place each pretzel on the oiled baking sheet after shaping.

Put 350ml water in a large covered saucepan, add the bicarbonate of soda and bring to the boil. Use a slotted spoon or a flat sieve to lower five of the pretzels (or fewer, depending on your pan size) in to the boiling water. Boil for 30 seconds then use tongs to turn each pretzel over gently and boil for a further 30 seconds. Drain each boiled pretzel well by gently shaking it while holding over the water, then place back on the oiled baking sheet and sprinkle with a generous amount of salt and/or seeds (if using) while still damp. Bake the salted/seeded pretzels on the upper shelf of the oven for 12-15 minutes until they are firm and glossy brown.

Allow to cool on a wire rack. These taste best on the day they're baked, so simply freeze any pretzels that don't get eaten straight away for future use – just refresh in a 150°C/130°C fan/gas mark 2 oven for 5-10 minutes for freshly baked pretzels whenever you want them.

Soft polar flatbread

You can find soft flatbreads all over the globe and they make fantastic wraps. If you bake them a little longer, they can also make crunchy, crisp accompaniments to salads or soups. The soft ones keep for about 3-4 days in an airtight container – just refresh them in the oven if they need softening up. The crisp ones keep much longer and are great to have on standby for when you don't have time to bake.

MAKES TWO LARGE FLATBREADS

250g whole milk
50g butter
400g refined spelt (or plain) flour
100g wholemeal spelt (or wheat) flour
2 tsp fine sea salt
15g fresh yeast or 7g fast action dried yeast
1 tsp caster sugar (if using fresh yeast)
flaky sea salt for garnishing (optional)

Scald the milk by heating it in a small pan with the butter until it is almost boiling and then allow it to cool while you assemble the other ingredients. Scalding the milk makes the finished bread softer.

Sift the flours and salt together in a large bowl, sprinkle in the dried yeast (if using) and stir through. If using fresh yeast, cream it with a teaspoon of sugar in a small bowl and once it is liquid (after about 30 seconds), add to the dry ingredients.

Make a well in the middle of the dry ingredients and add the scalded milk, which should be warm rather than hot to the touch, as otherwise you risk killing the yeast. Stir everything together until the mixture comes off the sides of the bowl and looks – for want of a better word – doughy.

Once the dough comes together and starts to feel springy, leave it to rise in a warm place for 45-60 minutes or until it has more or less doubled in size. Lightly oil two rectangular baking sheets and then tip out and knock back the dough. Divide it in to two and place half on each baking sheet. Using your hands squish and spread the dough out in to each corner of the baking sheet. Don't worry about it being perfectly smooth, the more lumpy and rustic it looks the better! Cover with lightly oiled clingfilm or a teatowel and leave to prove for a further 15-30 minutes or so, then press with your little finger to check for spring back – if the indentation stays in place, your flatbread is ready to be baked.

Preheat the oven to 220°C/200°C fan/gas mark 7. Brush the flatbreads with water and scatter sea salt flakes (if using) over the top. Splash a little water in the bottom of the oven to create steam to help the bread to rise. Place one baking sheet on the top shelf of the oven and bake for 7-8 minutes – it should still look pale and feel soft to the touch.

(If you prefer a crunchy flatbread, bake for a further 10 minutes until it feels crisp, turning the heat down to 200°C/180°C fan/gas mark 6 or 190°C/170°C fan/ gas mark 5 if the bread is taking on a bit too much colour.)

Leave the soft- or crunchy-cooked flatbread to cool on a wire rack while you bake the other half of the dough. (You can bake both batches at the same time if you have a fan-assisted oven which heats evenly throughout, but I tend to get more consistent results baking in single batches.)

VARIATIONS

If you want to flavour the flatbread, try adding a tablespoon of caraway, fennel and/ or anise seeds to the dry ingredients.

Poppy and sesame seeds are great additions – sprinkle either or both liberally over the flatbread with the salt before baking.

A handful of grated cheese sprinkled on top before baking makes a great-tasting flatbread too.

Crunchy mixed seed and rosemary flatbread

Crisp flatbreads are enormously popular across Scandinavia to eat whenever you feel peckish or haven't got fresh bread in the house. I love eating them as mid-afternoon snacks or with a bowl of hot vegetable soup in autumn and winter. You can make yeasted flatbreads of course, but these are unleavened for a faster flatbread. The seeds add essential fatty acids and a satisfying crunch, while the rosemary adds a hint of extra flavour.

MAKES 4 TRAYS OF FLATBREAD

150g refined spelt (or plain) flour
150g wholemeal spelt (or wheat) flour
100g rye flour
50g oat bran
1½ tsp fine sea salt
3 tbsp melted butter or vegetable oil

200-250ml whole milk
5 tbsp mixed seeds (e.g. sesame seeds, linseed, flaxseed, poppy seeds)
2 tbsp caraway seeds
1 tbsp anise seeds
2 tbsp finely chopped fresh rosemary
2-3 tsp flaky sea salt (to taste)

Line two baking trays with baking parchment.

This dough can be made by hand or in a mixer. Mix the flours, bran and salt together with the melted butter or oil. Slowly add the milk until the mixture comes together and starts to look like dough. Stop adding milk as soon as this happens – if you add too much the dough will be sticky, making it tricky to roll out.

Tip the dough out on to a lightly floured surface and quickly knead for a minute until it looks smooth and feels soft. Divide it in four balls and flatten each piece in a small disc about 10cm across. Wrap each one in clingfilm and refrigerate for 45 minutes (or pop in the freezer for 15-20 minutes). The more you chill the dough, the crisper your flatbread will be.

Preheat the oven to 220°C/200°C fan/gas mark 7. Mix all the seeds, the rosemary and the flaky sea salt together in a bowl – I quite like a salty topping so I use up to three teaspoonsful of salt, but feel free to use less. When you're ready to roll out the flatbread, take half of it out of the fridge or freezer, leaving the remaining two dough rounds to stay cool.

Sprinkle a quarter of the seed mixture on to each baking tray, then roll out a round of dough on top of the seeds, turning the dough one quarter clockwise after each roll until it is about 2mm thick. The seeds will spill around the edges as you roll, so just keep sweeping them back under the dough. If the dough starts to stick to the rolling pin, sprinkle a little flour on top of the dough and rub some on your rolling pin. The thinner the rolled dough, the crispier it will be when baked, so it's worth being patient. Repeat the seeding and rolling process with the other round of dough.

Pop both trays in the oven and bake for 4 minutes before swapping the two trays around (so that they bake evenly) and cooking for another 3-4 minutes. Keep an eye on the flatbread – it can very quickly go from being pale and a little underdone to dark and a little overdone! Remove the flatbread from the oven, tip on to a wire rack and leave to cool.

Run cold water over the trays to cool them, then dry them so they are ready for the second batch. Repeat the seeding, rolling and baking process with the remaining two rounds of dough.

If you are concerned about the crispbread burning, you can always take it out while it is still a little pale, cool it, break in to shards and then place on the racks in a 150°C/130°C fan/gas mark 2 oven for 15-20 minutes to really crisp up. Do the same if you find the flatbreads are still a little soft once cooled. These flatbreads should keep in an airtight container for up to a month.

Other topping suggestions to sprinkle on the baking tray before you roll out the dough:

freshly ground black or pink peppercorns
finely grated cheese
a mixture of fennel seeds, cayenne pepper, chilli, cumin seeds, ground allspice and/
or coriander seeds

Crisp oat bran flatbread
with cardamom sugar

This sweet, light flatbread has a fabulous cardamom crunch, perfect for mid-morning elevenses or for a mini snack with a cup of tea. For a more indulgent treat, dip in hot chocolate, warm chocolate sauce or chocolate hazelnut spread.

MAKES 4 TRAYS OF FLATBREAD

400g refined spelt (or plain) flour
50g oat bran
1 tsp fine sea salt
2 tbsp melted butter or vegetable oil
200-225ml whole milk
150g caster sugar
2 tsp ground cardamom

Line two baking trays with baking parchment.

This dough can be made by hand or in a mixer. Mix the flour, bran and salt together with the melted butter or oil. Slowly add the milk until the mixture comes together and starts to look like dough. Stop adding milk as soon as this happens – if you add too much the dough will be sticky, making it tricky to roll out.

Tip the dough out on to a lightly floured surface and quickly knead the dough for a minute until it looks smooth and feels soft. Divide it in four balls and flatten each piece in to a small disc about 10cm across. Wrap each one in clingfilm and refrigerate for 45 minutes (or pop in the freezer for 15-20 minutes). The more you chill the dough, the crisper your flatbread will be.

Preheat the oven to 220°C/200°C fan/gas mark 7. Mix the caster sugar and cardamom together in a bowl, stirring so the spice distributes evenly throughout the sugar. When you're ready to roll out the flatbread, take half of it out of the fridge or freezer, leaving the remaining two dough rounds to stay cool.

Sprinkle a quarter of the cardamom mixture on to a baking tray, then roll out a round of dough on top of the seeds, turning the dough one quarter clockwise after each roll until it is about 2mm thick. The sugar will spill around the edges as you roll so just keep sweeping it back under the dough. If the dough starts to stick to the rolling pin, simply sprinkle a little flour on top and rub some on your rolling pin. The thinner the rolled dough, the crispier it will be when baked so it's worth being patient. Repeat the sugaring and rolling process with the other round of dough.

Pop both trays in the oven and bake for 4 minutes before swapping the two trays around (so that they bake evenly) and cooking for another 3-4 minutes. Keep an eye on the flatbread – it can very quickly go from being pale and a little underdone to dark and a little overdone! Remove the flatbread from the oven, tip on to a wire rack and leave to cool. Run cold water over the trays to cool them, then dry them so they are ready for the second batch. Repeat the sugaring, rolling and baking process with the remaining two rounds of dough.

If you are concerned about burning, you can always take the crispbread out while it is still a little pale, cool it, break in to shards and then place on the racks in a 150°C/130°C fan/gas mark 2 oven for 15-20 minutes to really crisp up. Do the same if you find the flatbreads are still a little soft once cooled. These flatbreads should keep in an airtight container for up to a month.

Other topping suggestions to sprinkle on the baking tray
before you roll out the dough:
 cinnamon sugar
 mixed spice sugar
 zesty rosehip sugar, using about 130g sugar and 30g ground dried rosehips

Flavoured butters

Flavoured butters are great on open sandwiches, melted on to hot dishes or simply as an alternative to ordinary butter at the lunch or dinner table. They're also fantastic to have on standby for everything from speedy suppers to cooking emergencies, so if you're not intending to use the butter straight away, tip it on to a large sheet of clingfilm and roll up in a tight sausage. Seal the ends well to ensure that the butter is completely airtight and store in the fridge for 4-5 days or in the freezer for up to 1 month. That way, it'll be ready to use whenever you need it…

Horseradish and lemon butter

This is brilliant on open sandwiches with grilled mackerel, hot smoked trout or smoked salmon. It's also really good melted on roasted fish, grilled vegetables and chicken dishes.

125g unsalted butter, softened
3 tbsp hot horseradish sauce
zest and juice of 1 lemon
1 tsp freshly cracked white pepper
½ – ¾ tsp fine sea salt

Cream the butter with a wooden spoon for 10-15 seconds until it's really soft, then add the remaining ingredients and taste; it should be quite hot and citrussy. Feel free to add more horseradish, lemon juice or seasoning to taste – you want this butter to pack a real punch.

Anchovy and dill butter

This is delicious on baked eggs, sourdough toast with soft boiled egg and dabbed on top of Jansson's Temptation (Scandinavian anchovy and potato gratin). It also works beautifully on fish, lamb and steamed new potatoes.

125g unsalted butter, softened
100g tin of *Abba* anchovies
15g bunch fresh dill
¼ tsp fine sea salt

Cream the butter with a wooden spoon for 10-15 seconds until it's really soft. Drain the anchovies and blitz with the butter in a small food processor or using a handheld blender. Add the dill and salt, then blitz again until the dill is finely chopped and everything is well combined.

If you don't have a blender, finely chop the anchovies and the dill before combining with the butter and sea salt.

Caraway and coriander butter

This butter works really well with a wide variety of fish, meat and game. I love to put it on root vegetables when they are oven-roasting too.

1 tbsp caraway seeds
1 tbsp coriander seeds
125g unsalted butter, softened
½ tsp freshly cracked black pepper
½–¾ tsp fine sea salt

Toast the caraway and coriander seeds for a couple of minutes in a pan over a low-medium heat. The toasting will help release the flavour of the seeds, but do make sure you don't burn them or they'll taste acrid. Allow the spices to cool.

Cream the butter with a wooden spoon for 10-15 seconds until it's really soft. Blitz the butter, spices and seasoning in a small food processor or using a handheld blender until everything is well combined.

If you don't have a blender, grind the spices to a fine powder in a pestle and mortar before combining with the butter and seasoning.

Cinnamon and vanilla butter

Use this on your toast in the morning, on sweet open sandwiches with sliced strawberries or ripe nectarines, or melted and drizzled over pancakes, waffles or French toast.

125g unsalted butter, softened
75g caster sugar
1 tbsp cinnamon
1 tsp vanilla sea salt

Cream the butter with a wooden spoon for 10-15 seconds until it's really soft. Add the remaining ingredients and mix well, or blitz in a small food processor or using a handheld blender until everything is fully combined.

Jams

Strawberry freezer jam

We always made a lot of frysetøy, *or freezer jam, when I was growing up in Norway, and I love it. In fact, I once told my grandmother that I preferred my dad's freezer strawberry jam to her cooked strawberry jam and I don't think she ever really forgave me! Freezer jam is similar to compote, but with a fresher flavour and lots of nice big pieces of berry. It works fantastically with strawberries, blueberries, raspberries and blackberries but I tend to avoid thicker-skinned fruit like cherries and plums. The amount of fructose you use will vary depending on how ripe the berries are: 375g fructose if they're perfectly ripe; 450-500g if they are tart and under-ripe. The pectin helps the strawberries to set – use both sachets if you like a firm set jam, or just the one if you prefer a loose set, as I do.*

MAKES ABOUT 2.5 LITRES

2kg strawberries, hulled and quartered
375-500g fructose (or 560-750g caster sugar)

juice of 1 lemon
1–2 sachets of pectin (13-26g), optional

Place the strawberries in a large bowl or saucepan. Sprinkle the fructose over the fruit, add the juice of a lemon, and a sachet or two of pectin (if using). Stir through using a large metal spoon until the strawberries start to macerate and ooze juice – be patient as this may take a few minutes. Decant in to freezeable plastic tubs or boxes and then freeze. Easy.

When you want to use the freezer jam, simply take it out of the freezer the night before and leave in the fridge to defrost slowly until you're ready to spread some on your toast the next morning.

Sour cherry jam

There were four or five sour cherry trees on my grandparents' farm near the west coast of Norway and we loved picking (and eating) them in July. Sour cherries are wonderful eaten fresh from the tree, plus they make the most fantastic crimson cherry jam and compote, eaten as it is or folded through with lightly whipped cream to make a tangy fruit fool. Darker, sweet cherries are great too of course, but there's something really special about sour cherries so if you have a local supply do make good use of it. And investing in a cherry pitter would be a really good idea too… This loose set jam is slightly tart, so feel free to add more sugar to taste.

MAKES 10-12 JARS (227ML EACH)

2kg de-pitted cherries
200ml water

400g fructose
juice of 1 lemon

Preheat the oven to 100°C/80°C fan/gas mark ¼ while you wash the jam jars, then pop them in the oven for 10 minutes to dry and sterilise them. Stand them upside down on a clean tea towel until you need them. Meanwhile place a small saucer in the freezer for testing how set the jam is.

Put the cherries and the water in a large heavy-based saucepan over a medium heat, stirring fairly regularly while the fruit starts to disintegrate and cook, ensuring that it doesn't catch on the bottom of the pan and burn. When the mixture starts to look bright red like a rough tomato soup, bring it to the boil and then stir thoroughly. Repeat this twice, so that you have brought it to the boil three times in total. My father taught me this method and while I am never quite sure whether it's deeply scientific or simply superstitious about the number 3, it does always seem to work.

Take the pan off the heat, add the fructose and stir really well to distribute it. Put the pan back on the heat and bring to the boil again before adding the lemon juice. Remove from the heat and test the jam by placing a dollop on the frozen saucer and swirling it around. The jam should neither be runny nor too jellified. If you're not sure, try drawing your finger across the surface of the jam on the saucer – if it wrinkles then the jam is ready. If not, then boil for another 5 minutes before checking again.

Decant in to the sterilised jars, seal and turn upside down until cool. Turning the jam jars upside down while they cool reduces the chance of any rogue bacteria getting in to the air above the jam surface while it is cooling. Store the filled jam jars in a cool, dry place and once opened keep in the fridge.

Serve with almond cake, or on its own with toast, on top of plain yoghurt or with some ice cream. Heavenly.

Greengage and vanilla jam

Reine Claudes, or greengages as they're more commonly known, are pretty, pale green plums that you get towards the end of July and in to August. My Norwegian grandparents grew them on their farm and my dad and I adore them. They have quite a subtle flavour, tending towards a juicy, honeyed sweetness when they're perfectly ripe. Considered the king of dessert plums, these are fantastic baked in cakes, stewed as breakfast compote or cooked in a sticky jam like this one. Greengage has a natural affinity with vanilla so I've added a pod here for extra aroma but by all means feel free to omit if you'd rather.

MAKES 10-12 JARS (227ML EACH)

2kg de-stoned ripe greengages, quartered
200ml water
1 vanilla pod, split

350g fructose (plus more if needed)
juice of 1 lemon

Preheat the oven to 100°C/80°C fan/gas mark ¼ while you wash the jam jars, then pop them in the oven for 10 minutes to dry and sterilise them. Stand them upside down on a clean tea towel until you need them. Meanwhile place a small saucer in the freezer for testing how set the jam is.

Put the greengages and the water in a large heavy-based saucepan over a medium heat, scrape the vanilla pod clean of its seeds in to the saucepan and toss in the vanilla pod too. Stirring fairly regularly while the fruit starts to disintegrate and cook, ensure that the jam doesn't catch on the bottom of the pan and burn. When the mixture starts to look like mustard-yellow fruity soup, bring it to the boil and then stir thoroughly. Repeat this twice, so that you have brought it to the boil three times in total. My father taught me this method and while I am never quite sure whether it's deeply scientific or simply superstitious about the number 3, it does always seem to work.

Take the pan off the heat, add the fructose (you may need to add a little more than 350g if the greengages aren't fully ripe) and stir really well to distribute it. Put the pan back on the heat and bring to the boil again before adding the lemon juice. Remove from the heat and test the jam by placing a dollop on the frozen saucer and swirling it around. The jam should neither be runny or nor too jellified. If you're not sure, try drawing your finger across the surface of the jam on the saucer – if it wrinkles then the jam is ready. If not, then boil for another 5 minutes before checking again.

Remove the split vanilla pod before decanting the jam in to the sterilised jars, seal and turn upside down until cool. Turning the jam jars upside down while they cool reduces the chance of any rogue bacteria getting in to the air above the jam surface while it is cooling. Store the filled jam jars in a cool, dry place and once opened keep in the fridge.

Gooseberry and elderflower jam

Gooseberries, or stikkelsbær *in Norwegian, are widely available across Scandinavia. Their Norwegian name means 'prickly berries', an accurate description for this bristly little fruit. Gooseberries vary according to the season – early season ones tend to be small and green and are ideal for cooking, while later season gooseberries are larger and sweeter, making for better eating, and they can be yellow, green or pink-red. Taste yours before you start making this jam, as you may need more fructose if they are very tart. Gooseberries and elderflower complement each other beautifully, each lifting the other's flavour to make something really rather elegant.*

MAKES 10-12 JARS (227ML EACH)

2kg gooseberries,
    topped, tailed
    and halved
200ml water

100ml elderflower cordial
    or syrup (plus more if needed)
250g fructose
juice of 1 lemon

Preheat the oven to 100°C/80°C fan/gas mark ¼ while you wash the jam jars, then pop them in the oven for 10 minutes to dry and sterilise them. Stand them upside down on a clean tea towel until you need them. Meanwhile place a small saucer in the freezer for testing how set the jam is.

Put the gooseberries and the water in a large heavy-based saucepan over a medium heat, and start stirring fairly regularly while the fruit starts to disintegrate and cook, ensuring that the jam doesn't catch on the bottom of the pan and burn. When the gooseberries' skins start deflating and the seeds start mixing together, bring the mixture to the boil and then stir thoroughly. Repeat this twice, so that you have brought it to the boil three times in total. My father taught me this method and while I am never quite sure whether it's deeply scientific or simply superstitious about the number 3, it does always seem to work.

Take the pan off the heat, add the elderflower cordial and fructose and stir really well to distribute it. Taste and see if the elderflower flavour is strong enough – this will depend on the strength of the cordial – and add more if necessary.

Put the pan back on the heat and bring to the boil again before adding the lemon juice. Remove from the heat and test the jam by placing a dollop on the frozen saucer and swirling it around. Draw your finger across the surface of the jam on the saucer – if it wrinkles then the jam is ready. If not, then boil for another 5 minutes before checking again.

Decant the gooseberry and elderflower jam in to the sterilised jars, seal and turn upside down until cool. Turning the jam jars upside down while they cool reduces the chance of any rogue bacteria getting in to the air above the jam surface while it is cooling. Store the filled jam jars in a cool, dry place and once opened keep in the fridge.

Open sandwiches

Strawberries and granola

A healthier riff on indulgent French toast, this strawberry sandwich ticks all the boxes – a little fibre, a little fruit, a little protein and a little something sweet. Fruity, creamy and delicious, it's perfect for those summer mornings when you want something special to start your day.

SERVES 2

200g strawberries, washed, hulled and quartered
2–3 tbsp fructose
4 thin slices rye bread
cinnamon and vanilla butter (p. 51)
200g fromage frais, quark or greek yoghurt
maple syrup for drizzling
30g almond flakes
40g spiced crispy rye granola (p. 168)

Start by mixing the strawberries with two tablespoons of the fructose in a small bowl. Taste and add the remaining fructose if you think the strawberries need it, depending on how ripe they are (and how sweet a tooth you have). Leave them to macerate while you toast the rye bread to crisp it up. Spread the cinnamon and vanilla butter on the hot toast, and then add a dollop of fromage frais or other creamy topping. Pile on the macerated strawberries, drizzle with maple syrup and scatter the almond flakes on top, along with the crispy granola. Eat immediately.

Hot smoked trout with radish, lemon and horseradish

Hot smoked trout is readily available in supermarkets and delis these days, but leftover cooked salmon works well in this sandwich too. Equally, if you don't have any sorrel, just use mint, parsley or chives instead. Nutritious and full of contrasting flavours and textures, this makes a delightful spring or summer lunch for eating outdoors (weather permitting!)

SERVES 2

butter, softened
2 slices barley bread (see page 16) or sourdough
1 tbsp hot horseradish sauce
125g hot smoked trout
4 radishes, sliced

2 sorrel leaves, shredded
zest and juice of ½ lemon
a couple of dollops of crème fraîche (optional)

Butter the bread and spread horseradish on each slice. Flake the trout and divide between the bread slices. Decorate with radish, scatter with sorrel, sprinkle on some lemon zest and spritz a little juice over the top for good measure. A dollop of crème fraîche on each slice is delicious too, but is not essential. Eat immediately.

Crab and asparagus

One of the great joys of going to the fish market in Bergen, on the west coast of Norway, is eating a freshly cooked, dressed crab. It's usually the first thing my father does when he returns to his hometown. I have fairly traditional views about how to dress crab, with its delicate flesh with a hint of sweetness and a hint of salt from the sea. This is an easy and foolproof – if rather luxurious – open sandwich, best eaten freshly made (dressed crab doesn't travel well in your rucksack!)

SERVES 1

2 small thin asparagus spears
1 small cooked crab (white and dark meat)
1-2 tbsp mayonnaise
1 tbsp soured cream
1 tbsp salad cream
zest and juice of ½ lemon
1 sprig dill, finely chopped
½ shallot, thinly sliced
1 large slice sourdough bread
butter, softened
borage flowers (optional)

Blanch the asparagus in boiling water for half a minute. Mix the crab meat with the mayonnaise, soured cream and salad cream. Stir in the zest, dill and shallot, and season to taste with salt and white pepper. Cut the blanched asparagus stalks in thin slices on the diagonal.

Toast the sourdough and spread with a generous layer of butter, then add the crab mixture and gently smooth down. Scatter the asparagus over the top, squeeze a little lemon juice on the sandwich and garnish with a few borage flowers, if using. Serve immediately.

Grilled cheese, mushroom and hazelnut

Grilled cheese is my favourite guilty pleasure. I am perfectly capable of devouring indecent quantities with a variety of different toppings in one sitting. The key elements to this tasty sandwich are: good cheese, good bread, good fresh mushrooms and a grill that works. Diced cooked bacon makes a delicious addition too. I like to eat this as a simple lunch or supper with a green salad alongside. You can ring the flavour changes by sprinkling spices on to the cheese before grilling – try cumin, cayenne, ground allspice or white pepper. If you fancy adding herbs instead, rosemary and thyme can be sprinkled on the cheese before grilling, while parsley and oregano are more delicate and should be added afterwards.

SERVES TWO

150g mushrooms, sliced
25g butter, plus more for spreading
1 tsp fresh tarragon, finely chopped
1 tsp caraway seeds
20g hazelnuts, halved or chopped
2 slices sourdough bread
approx. 100g Jarlsberg, Gouda, *Västerbotten* and/or
  Havarti cheese with caraway
a few drops Worcestershire sauce (optional)

Sauté the mushrooms in the butter over a high heat so that they reduce and brown quickly. Season to taste with salt and pepper, then sprinkle with the tarragon, caraway seeds and hazelnuts, cooking for a further minute so all the flavours infuse together.

Toast the sourdough on one side, butter the non-toasted side and divide the cooked mushrooms between the toast. Shave cheese slices on top until all the mushroom is covered. I like a thick layer of cheese but then I am a cheese fiend. Sprinkle a little Worcester sauce over the cheese (if using).

Put under a medium-hot grill until bubbling and golden brown. Serve immediately.

Savouries

When you mention baking,

many people think only of bread, cakes and biscuits, and they forget the mouth-watering cheese, fish, meat and vegetable-filled baked delights which take centre stage at picnics, lunches and suppers.

The Scandinavian countries have some marvellous cheeses (old favourites like *Västerbotten*, Jarslberg and Havarti, as well as delicious artisan cheeses) and a good thing too, as we eat cheese at breakfast, lunch and dinner! It is also fantastic to bake with – whether as cheese straws, melt-in-the-mouth *sablé* biscuits, pumpkin, cheese and sage muffins or baked cheese and onion cheesecake.

Long-standing maritime traditions and extensive coastlines mean that seafood also plays a major role in Scandi cuisine, and in my baking. Tasty *Abba* anchovies give a savoury twist to cheese straws and cauliflower cheese, garlicky crayfish provides a heavenly filling for buttery filo bites, crab lends its delicate flavour to asparagus tart, and hearty fishes like cod and salmon star as the main features in creamy fish pie and crispy bakes.

Vegetables are great for making delicious healthy savoury dishes, whether using sweet summery peas, beans and asparagus, or cold-weather favourites like cauliflower, broccoli, mushrooms, carrots and pumpkin. Roasted cauliflower, anchovy and crème fraîche bake makes a fabulous supper for a frosty winter's night and wild mushrooms (foraged or bought) are delicious in a creamy herby tart.

I hope that these recipes will whet your appetite and inspire you to try out some great-tasting savoury dishes – from traditional egg-butter covered Karelian rice pies to my somewhat unorthodox *Scandilicious* meatball buns! Sounds crazy I know, but I just couldn't resist…

Abba anchovy cheese straws
Västerbotten and caraway *sablés*
Crayfish filo bites
Jarlsberg and ale buns
Pumpkin, cheese and sage muffins
Meatball buns
Cheese and onion cheesecake
Wild mushroom tart
Crab and asparagus tart
Scandilicious fish gratin
Roasted cauliflower,
  anchovy and crème fraîche bake
Crispy baked salmon
Karelian pies

Abba anchovy cheese straws

I have an incurable addiction to Abba *anchovies, the soft little Swedish sprats in a spiced sweet-saline brine. I love them spread on buttered toast to dunk in a soft-boiled egg, scatter through Jansson's Temptation (Scandinavian anchovy and potato bake) and as a flavour enhancer in lots of savoury dishes. These anchovy and cheese twists are just another manifestation of my enduring love of* Abba *(the anchovies and the pop group).*

MAKES 25-30

375g ready-made all butter puff pastry
1 medium egg, beaten
125g tin of *Abba* anchovies, drained
75g finely grated *Västerbotten* cheese, plus more for sprinkling (optional)

Roll the pastry in to a rectangle about 3mm thick and brush the surface lightly with egg. Mash the anchovies in to a paste. Spread half the anchovies on the pastry and scatter half the cheese over the top. Fold the pastry in half and roll out until it is about 3mm thick again. Brush the surface lightly with a little more egg and then spread the remaining anchovies and cheese over it. Fold the pastry in half again and roll out to the same thickness as before. Seal the edges of your cheesy-anchovy pastry, brush the surface one final time with the egg, place on a baking sheet, cover with clingfilm and refrigerate for 30-45 minutes.

Preheat the oven to 200°C/180°C fan/gas mark 6 and line a baking sheet with parchment paper. Take the pastry sheet out of the fridge, lay it flat on the worksurface and use a sharp knife to cut it in long strips about 1cm wide. Twist the pastry strips several times from both ends to give a spiral shape. Place the pastry twists on the baking sheet with a good few centimetres between each one as they will puff up during cooking. Sprinkle on extra cheese if you wish.

Bake for 7-9 minutes or until golden and flaky to the touch. Allow to cool on a wire rack, or serve warm from the oven if (like me) you can't wait that long!

Västerbotten and caraway *sablés*

Savoury cheese biscuits, or sablés, *are great nibbles when you're having friends over for drinks or at a cocktail party. They're also great in picnic or lunch boxes for a little savoury snack. Scandinavians love their cheese, and* Västerbotten's *nutty, crystalline texture is reminiscent of Italian Parmigiano, making it a perfect ingredient to cook and bake with. The caraway adds an aromatic crunch but feel free to omit it or replace with other seeds – for example coriander, fennel or cumin.*

MAKES ABOUT 20

110g refined spelt (or plain) flour
¼ tsp fine sea salt
55g butter, very cold
75g *Västerbotten* cheese, finely grated
1 medium egg, lightly beaten, plus more to glaze
1-2 tbsp whole milk
2-3 tsp caraway seeds

Line a baking sheet with parchment or greaseproof paper.

Blitz the flour, salt and butter together in a blender until everything resembles breadcrumbs. If you do this by hand (which obviously will take longer than if using a blender) do make sure the butter is extremely cold – the colder the butter, the better the *sablé*.

Add the grated cheese to the mixture, then add the egg and one tablespoon of milk and bring everything together. If need be, add the rest of the milk (or a little water) and bring the dough together in 3 or 4 pulses of the mixer, or light kneading if using your hands – overhandling the dough risks making the pastry tough.

Roll in to a long sausage shape with a diameter of roughly 3cm and wrap tightly with clingfilm. Chill in the freezer for 10-15 minutes (or in the fridge for about 45 minutes) until firm and very cold.

Preheat the oven to 200°C/180°C fan/gas mark 6. Remove the *sablé* dough from the freezer/fridge, unwrap the clingfilm and slice the dough in to 20 evenly-sized discs. Put the discs about 3-4cm apart on the lined baking sheet, brush with egg and sprinkle the caraway seeds on top. Bake in the oven for 8-10 minutes until the *sablés* look golden brown and feel firm to the touch.

Allow to cool on a wire rack and store in a tin or tupperware box once completely cool. Eat within 3-4 days.

✳ If you like your *sablés* extra cheesy, sprinkle a little more grated cheese on top of each disc with the caraway seeds before baking.

Crayfish filo bites

*These crispy buttery little bites were inspired by summers spent crayfish fishing in Norway.
Well it was my dad who did most of the fishing, but I loved having fjord-fresh crayfish cooked on
the barbecue, lightly brushed with a garlic-parsley butter. Crayfish parties are held outdoors in late
August and September in Scandinavia, particularly in Sweden, and it's a great way to bid adieu
to summer. Since it's often hard to get hold of fresh crayfish outside Scandinavia, I've used cooked
crayfish tails in this recipe.*

MAKES 12 CANAPÉ-SIZED BITES

60g butter
2 filo pastry sheets
1 clove garlic
small handful chopped parsley
1 tbsp lemon juice
150g cooked crayfish tails, roughly chopped

Preheat the oven to 200°C/180°C fan/gas mark 6. Melt 40g of the butter in a small
pan or in the microwave. Brush one filo sheet with half the melted butter. Slice this
sheet in to 12 squares and place each one in a small muffin tin / patty pan. Repeat
with the other sheet of filo pastry, placing the second buttered square diagonally on
top of the first one (i.e. turned 90°), so that you can see all 8 corners of the two filo
squares spaced evenly around the edges of each muffin cup.

Melt the remaining butter in a small saucepan and add the garlic, parsley and lemon
juice. Allow to cook for a minute or so before adding the crayfish tails, tossing them
to give a good coating, and season to taste. Gently dollop a spoonful of buttery crayfish
tails in to each filo pocket and scrunch the pastry edges together to make filo 'money-bag'
parcels, brushing with a little melted butter to seal the top.

Bake on the upper shelf of the oven for 10-12 minutes or until the pastry looks golden
and feels crisp to the touch. Check the bottom of the parcels when you take them out
of the oven – if they feel a little undercooked, simply pop the bites back on the lower
shelf of the oven on a wire rack for a minute or two more. Place the cooked parcels on
a couple of sheets of kitchen roll to absorb any excess butter, before serving and eating
while warm.

Jarlsberg and ale buns

I use Vintage Jarlsberg (also known as Reserve) for this recipe because it has a stronger, punchier flavour, but if you can't lay your hands on any, use regular Jarlsberg, Cheddar, Gruyère or Comté cheese. I like to sprinkle a mixture of linseed, pumpkin, hemp, poppy and sunflower seeds on top of these muffins to give them a nutty crunch. Do note that if you are going to be leaving the dough to ferment overnight in the fridge, you only need to use half the quantity of yeast specified below.

MAKES 12

200g refined spelt (or plain) flour
140g wholemeal spelt (or wheat) flour
15g fresh yeast or 7g fast action dried yeast
1 tsp salt
2 tbsp treacle (or clear honey)
250-290ml ale
45g butter, melted
approx. 100g Vintage Jarlsberg cheese, cut in 12 cubes (1-2cm²), plus more for grating
1 medium egg, beaten
mixed seeds (optional)
oat or spelt flakes (optional)

Lightly oil a 12-hole muffin tin. Sift the flours, dried yeast (if using) and salt together in a large bowl. If using fresh yeast, place it in a separate small bowl and add the treacle to it. The yeast will dissolve and fizz slightly.

Make a well in the middle of the bowl and add the treacle (or yeast-treacle mix, if using fresh yeast). Add about 250ml of the ale and the melted butter, holding back the rest of the ale to see if you have a wet dough or dry dough. Flours tend to vary in their capacity to absorb liquid so it's worth erring on the side of caution. You want the dough to feel tacky and soft when you touch it – if it feels dry and tough, add a little more ale.

Stir the dough vigorously with a large spoon for 5 minutes. You should feel the dough becoming more elastic as the gluten strands in the flour expand. Once the dough looks smooth, cover the bowl with a teatowel or some lightly oiled clingfilm and set aside in a warm place to rise for 30-45 minutes (or you could place it in a lightly oiled plastic bag in the fridge overnight for a slow ferment) until it is doubled in size and is springy to the touch. Be aware that if you keep the dough in a lightly oiled plastic bag in the fridge overnight, the carbon dioxide gas from fermentation will expand the bag so make sure you leave plenty of space around it.

If you proved the dough in the fridge overnight, allow it to return to room temperature for 30 minutes or so before knocking the dough back, either using your hands on a lightly floured surface or using a large spoon in the bowl (I think it's more fun with your hands but it's up to you).

Divide the dough in to 12 equal-sized pieces (either judging by eye or by weighing it), put a cube of Jarlsberg in to the middle of each one and then roll the dough lightly around in your hands so the cheese is fully encased. Place the buns in the muffin tin, cover with a lightly oiled sheet of clingfilm and leave until they have doubled in size – this will take about 15-20 minutes in a warm room, longer if the room is cool.

Preheat the oven to 200°C/180°C fan/gas mark 6. Give one of the buns a gentle nudge with your finger – they are ready to bake if the indentation left by your finger stays put and the dough doesn't spring back. Brush the buns with beaten egg and sprinkle with a generous layer of grated cheese, along with some seeds and oat/spelt flakes (if using).

Bake the buns on the top shelf of the oven for 15-20 minutes until they are golden brown and sound hollow if you tap the base with your finger. Remove from the oven and allow to cool on a wire rack for a few minutes before devouring. These buns taste best on the day they're baked but you can always freeze any that don't get eaten. Reheat in the oven wrapped in foil for 10 minutes at 150°C/130°C fan/gas mark 2, then remove foil and turn the heat up to 190°C/170°C fan/gas mark 5 for 5 minutes to get freshly baked, gooey Jarlsberg and ale buns whenever you fancy them.

Pumpkin, cheese and sage muffins

This is a fabulous use for pumpkin – it combines wonderfully with the cheese and sage to make a mouthwatering muffin. I find it easiest to use tinned pumpkin, although you can of course use roasted fresh pumpkin if you have some to hand. Swedish Västerbotten *cheese is wonderful in these, but Jarlsberg, Gouda, Cheddar, Parmesan or Gruyère would be delicious too. Perfect for lunchboxes or taking on long, rambling walks on brisk autumnal days.*

MAKES 12

> 125g refined spelt (or plain) flour
> 125g wholemeal spelt (or wheat) flour
> 3 tbsp oats, plus 30g for sprinkling
> 2 tbsp light muscovado sugar
> 2 tsp baking powder
> ¼ tsp bicarbonate of soda
> ½ tsp fine sea salt
> 1 tsp cayenne pepper
> 3 sprigs fresh sage, roughly torn
> 275g pumpkin purée
> 100ml plain yoghurt
> 50g butter, melted
> 2 medium eggs, beaten
> 1 tbsp English mustard
> 100g *Västerbotten*, finely grated, plus 30g coarsely grated for sprinkling

Preheat the oven to 190°C/170°C fan/gas mark 5 and line a large 12-hole muffin tin with little squares of parchment paper or paper muffin cases.

Put all the dry ingredients and the torn sage leaves in a large bowl and stir through with a large spoon to distribute the raising agents. Mix the pumpkin purée, yoghurt and melted butter together in a medium bowl, stir in the beaten egg and then mix in the mustard and finely grated *Västerbotten*.

Make a well in the middle of the dry ingredients and pour in the liquid ingredients. Stir through about 12 times with a large spoon, using figure-of-eight motions to reach the bottom of the bowl and mix everything together.

Using an ice cream scoop or a tablespoon place an equal amount of mixture in to each muffin case. They dome quite high when baking so you can be generous when filling the cases. Sprinkle the muffins with the coarsely grated *Västerbotten* and the extra oats.

Bake on the upper-middle shelf of the oven for 20-25 minutes or until the muffins look golden brown and feel quite firm to the touch. Eat while warm, or leave to cool on a wire rack to be put in lunchboxes or to accompany soup. What you don't use, simply freeze to enjoy another day. Reheat in the oven wrapped in foil for 10 minutes at 150°C/130°C fan/ gas mark 2, then remove foil and turn the heat up to 190°C/170°C fan/gas mark 5 for 5 minutes to give them a good crunchy crust.

Meatball buns

These are hardly traditional but I have a thing about buns stuffed with meatballs. They remind me a little of the steamed buns you get in dim sum restaurants and are great eaten on the day they're baked for picnics or school lunches. This recipe yields more meatball mixture than you need for the buns, but I've never seen a problem with having leftover meatballs for sandwiches or late-night snacks!

MAKES 12

1 batch sesame *rundstykker* dough
  (page 39)
1 tbsp vegetable oil
½ medium onion, peeled and
  finely chopped
1 tsp ground allspice
½ tsp ground nutmeg
½ tsp ground ginger
1 tbsp plain yoghurt

100ml whole milk
1½ slices (c. 55g) stale white bread,
  preferably sourdough
200g veal mince
200g lamb mince
1 medium egg yolk
1 tsp fine sea salt
¼ tsp white pepper
50g butter, melted

Follow the sesame *rundstykker* recipe up to and including the second proving. Prepare and grill the meatballs while the dough is proving.

Heat the oil in a pan and cook the onion over a low heat for 8-10 minutes until soft. Once the onion goes translucent, add the spices and fry for a minute, then set aside to cool. Mix the yoghurt in to the milk and then pour it over the bread in a small bowl. Make sure all the bread is moistened and leave until the liquid has been absorbed.

Preheat the grill to medium-high. Combine the cooked onion, mince, egg yolk and seasoning in a large bowl. Add the milk-soaked bread and use your hands to mix everything together. Fry a spoonful of the mixture and, once cooked, taste to check your seasoning, making any adjustments necessary. Then lightly roll a teaspoon of meatball mixture between your palms to form meatballs and grill for 6-10 minutes, turning them once halfway through. They should be golden but not completely cooked through, as they will continue to cook when shaped in the bun. When the meatballs are cooked, brush 12 of them liberally with melted butter, which will help keep them moist when baked.

Preheat the oven to 220°C/200°C fan/gas mark 7 and line a baking tray with parchment paper.

Take each ball of proved *rundstykker* dough and squash in to a flattened disc between your palms. Put a meatball in the middle of each one and fold the dough around it, enveloping the meatball so it is completely enclosed. Use a little water to seal the edges together so the buns don't leak during baking and place on the prepared baking tray.

Bake on the middle shelf for 10 minutes, turning the heat down to 190°C/170°C fan/ gas mark 5 after that time if the buns are taking on too much colour. Continue to bake for a further 15-20 minutes until they are golden brown. Remove from the oven and allow to cool on a wire rack for 10-15 minutes. Eat while still warm.

Cheese and onion cheesecake

Cheesecake doesn't need to be sweet to be satisfying. This is a great savoury dish for entertaining or for taking on picnics.

SERVES 8

75g oat crackers
75g porridge oats
½ tsp fine sea salt
¼ tsp white peppercorns, finely crushed
50g butter, melted
3 medium eggs, separated
100g quark (or fromage frais)
1 tbsp plain flour
150g full fat cream cheese
3 spring onions, finely chopped
150g *Västerbotten* cheese, finely grated

Preheat the oven to 160°C/140°C fan/gas mark 3 and chill a 23cm round Pyrex pie dish (or cake tin). Blitz the crackers, oats, salt and peppercorns in a food processor (or seal them in a plastic bag and bash with a rolling pin) until the mixture resembles breadcrumbs. Put in a bowl, add the melted butter, stir a few times and tip in to the base of the pie dish, pressing down firmly. Set aside to chill in the freezer for 15-20 minutes or in the fridge for 45 minutes to an 1 hour.

Beat the egg yolks with a pinch of salt in a large bowl (I use an electric whisk), then add the quark and a pinch of the flour. Beat again and add the cream cheese along with the remainder of the flour, the spring onions and the *Västerbotten* (reserving some to sprinkle on top of the cheesecake just before baking, if you fancy it). Season to taste with salt and black pepper. It should be quite highly seasoned at this stage as the whisked egg whites will dilute the flavour.

Beat the egg whites separately with another pinch of salt until stiff peaks form. Add one large spoonful of this to the cheesy egg yolk mixture to loosen it, then fold through the rest of the egg whites, being careful not to knock out all the air.

Spoon the cheesecake mixture in to the chilled pie dish, flatten the top with a pallet knife, sprinkle with the reserved *Västerbotten* (if using) and then bake in the middle of the oven for 30 minutes, or until the surface feels firm. Cheesecake shouldn't take on too much colour, so check after 25 minutes and if necessary turn the heat down 20°C or so. Leave to cool in the oven for an hour after turning the oven off.

Serve at room temperature with a green salad or some steamed vegetables for a light lunch or supper.

Wild mushroom tart

Sweden and Finland are famous for the abundance of wild mushrooms that grow in their forests, and foraging is a great autumnal pastime. Make this tart with the freshest wild mushrooms you can get your hands on (if you have a glut you can always dry some for use later in the year, as they add a wonderful depth of flavour to risottos, soups and sauces). Do make sure to chill the pastry before filling and baking – it makes a real difference to the crispness when baked. If you can't get hold of buttermilk, just add half a teaspoon of lemon juice or white wine/cider vinegar to 50ml whole milk to sour it.

SERVES 4 AS A MAIN COURSE, 6-8 AS A STARTER

200g refined spelt (or plain) flour
100g spelt flakes
½ tsp fine sea salt
100g butter, chilled, plus 20g for frying
50ml buttermilk
300g wild mushrooms
1 large onion, finely chopped
3 tbsp vegetable oil
1 clove garlic, finely crushed
2 tsp fresh parsley, chopped
1 tsp fresh tarragon, chopped
1 tsp chives, chopped
400ml crème fraîche
40g *Västerbotten* cheese, finely grated (optional)
3 medium egg yolks

You will need a 23cm pastry tin with a 4-5cm tall rim, or a 23cm springform cake tin.

Pulse the flour, spelt flakes, salt and chilled butter in a blender or food processor until the mixture resembles breadcrumbs. (I always make this pastry in a mixer, as you need to break down the spelt flakes. If you don't have one, you can seal the spelt flakes in a plastic bag and bash it with a rolling pin to pulverise them before putting in a large bowl with the sifted flour and salt and rubbing in the butter.) Add buttermilk and pulse (or mix) again a couple of times until it comes together. As soon as the mixture resembles a dough, tip it on to a large piece of clingfilm. Knead lightly and shape in to a disc about 12cm in diameter. Wrap in the clingfilm and freeze for 15-20 minutes (or leave in the fridge overnight until you're ready to assemble the tart).

Preheat the oven to 190°C/170°C fan/gas mark 5. Take the pastry out of the fridge or freezer (if it's been in longer than 20 minutes, leave it to return to room temperature for 5-10 minutes before rolling out) and remove the clingfilm. Place the pastry disc between two sheets of baking parchment and roll out, turning the pastry 45° clockwise after each roll to get an even circle.

Once the pastry is about 3mm thick, lift it on to the rolling pin and carefully lower in to the pastry case or baking tin. If you find the pastry is very sticky or has become too warm to handle, place it back in the freezer for a few minutes to firm up again. Take a small nugget of pastry from the edge where it overlaps the tin and use that to press the pastry right down in to the edges of the tin. Then trim the excess pastry from around the edges. You can use this to fill any cracks or gaps, and anything left over can be rolled again, cut in little disks and baked for 8-10 minutes at 200°C/180°C fan/gas mark 6 to make excellent biscuits for cheese!

Once you've filled all the gaps and cracks, prick the base of the pastry case with a fork, line with parchment paper, weigh down with rice or baking beans and bake on the midle shelf for 20-25 minutes or until golden brown. Set aside to cool while you prepare the filling.

Reduce the oven temperature to 170°C/150°C fan/gas mark 3-4. Carefully clean the mushrooms using a pastry brush or a piece of kitchen paper. Chop in equal-sized pieces about 0.5cm thick and set aside.

Sweat the onion in a tablespoon of oil along with a pinch of salt in a frying pan over a low-medium heat until soft and translucent. Add the garlic and fry for a further 30 seconds before tipping in to a bowl and setting aside. Put the remaining vegetable oil and the additional 20g butter in the frying pan over a medium-high heat until really sizzling, then fry the mushrooms (cooking them over a relatively high heat like this will help to evaporate their excess moisture and prevent them stewing in their own liquid). Keep tossing the mushrooms while frying for a good 4-5 minutes until golden brown and reduced in size. Add the chopped herbs, season with salt and pepper and remove from the heat.

Add the crème fraîche to the mushrooms and stir so that it warms through, stir in the cheese and then add the egg yolks, stirring again. Add the onion and garlic mixture and stir a final time before pouring in to the pastry case. Bake on the middle shelf of the oven for 25-30 minutes or until the filling has set and doesn't wobble any more when shaken (it will set further as it cools in the tin but you don't want the tart to be a runny goo, so be patient when baking).

Leave to cool in the tin for about 30 minutes before serving while still warm with a green salad or some steamed broccoli, peas or green beans.

Crab and asparagus tart

I absolutely adore crab – it's fabulous on a slice of buttered sourdough toast with just some mayonnaise and a slice or two of cucumber to keep it company, and perhaps a few borage leaves and flowers if you're feeling fancy. But crabmeat is so versatile it seems a shame to restrict its use to an open sandwich. Crab and asparagus is of course a classic Northern European combination and this tart is an easy way of showing off the best of both. I tend to use a 2:1 ratio of white to brown crabmeat, but feel free to vary this according to your preference. This tart is perfect picnic fare or for when you have friends or family coming round. If you can't get hold of buttermilk, just add half a teaspoon of lemon juice or white wine/cider vinegar to 50ml whole milk to sour it.

SERVES 6

200g refined spelt
  (or plain) flour
½ tsp fine sea salt
100g butter, chilled
50ml buttermilk
350g crabmeat
bunch green or white asparagus
  (approx. 300g)

200g crème fraîche
2 medium eggs
1 medium egg yolk
1 tsp finely chopped chervil, parsley,
  chive or dill (optional)
zest of ½ lemon
¼ nutmeg, freshly grated

You will need a 23cm pastry tin with a 4-5cm tall rim, or a 23cm springform cake tin.

You can make this pastry by hand or in a mixer. Pulse the flour, salt and butter in a blender or food processor (or sift the dry ingredients in to a large bowl and rub in the butter) until the mixture resembles breadcrumbs. Add buttermilk and pulse (or mix) again a couple of times until it comes together. As soon as the mixture resembles a dough, tip it on to a large piece of clingfilm. Knead lightly and shape in to a disc about 12cm in diameter. Wrap in the clingfilm and freeze for 15-20 minutes (or leave in the fridge overnight until you're ready to assemble the tart).

Preheat the oven to 190°C/170°C fan/gas mark 5. Take the pastry out of the fridge or freezer (if it's been in longer than 20 minutes, leave it to return to room temperature for 5-10 minutes before rolling out) and remove the clingfilm. Place the pastry disc between two sheets of baking parchment and roll out, turning the pastry 45° clockwise after each roll to get an even circle.

Once the pastry is roughly 3mm thick, lift it on to the rolling pin and carefully lower in to the pastry case or baking tin. If you find the pastry is very sticky or has become too warm to handle, place it back in the freezer for a few minutes to firm up again. Take a small nugget of pastry from the edge where it overlaps the tin and use that to press the pastry right down in to the edges of the tin. Then trim the excess pastry from around the edges. You can use this to fill any cracks or gaps, and anything left over can be rolled again, cut in little disks and baked for 8-10 minutes at 200°C/180°C fan/gas mark 6 to make excellent biscuits for cheese!

Once you've filled all the gaps and cracks, prick the base of the pastry case with a fork, line with parchment paper, weigh down with rice or baking beans and bake on the middle shelf for 20-25 minutes or until golden brown. Set aside to cool while you prepare the filling. Reduce the oven temperature to 170°C/150°C fan/gas mark 3-4. Check through the crabmeat to see that there aren't any bits of shell or evidence of the delightfully named 'dead man's fingers' (crab lungs) as they can make you very ill. Boil the asparagus in salted water for 1 minute, refresh with ice cold water and slice in little-finger length pieces. In a medium bowl mix together the crab, the asparagus pieces and all the remaining ingredients, and season with salt and white pepper then pour in to the pastry case. Bake on the middle shelf of the oven for 25-30 minutes or until the filling no longer wobbles and feels set when you touch the surface of the tart (it will set further as it cools in the tin but you don't want the tart to be a runny goo, so be patient when baking).

Leave to cool in the tin for about 30 minutes before serving while still warm, ideally with a watercress salad or some cooked peas and greens, preferably sitting outside somewhere sunny.

Scandilicious fish gratin

Fiskegrateng, or fish gratin, is real comfort food. It is also a genius way of using up leftover salt cod or other fish if, like my Norwegian grandmother Oddny, you tend to overcater. Whenever we visited my grandparents' house in Bergen, she would prepare a slap-up celebratory salt cod meal to greet us on arrival, and the next night everyone would eagerly await the delicious fish gratin she would rustle up. There was never a risk that we wouldn't have fish gratin the next night, as there was always *leftover cod – my grandmother found it impossible to cook for small numbers, preferring instead to empty Bergen's best fishmonger of all its cod whenever the family arrived!*

SERVES 4 AS A MAIN COURSE OR 6-8 AS A STARTER

1 tbsp vegetable oil
1 tbsp butter, plus 25g for sauce and more to finish
1 leek, finely chopped
1 large onion, finely chopped
200ml crème fraîche
400ml milk
½ nutmeg, freshly grated
4 allspice berries
about 450g white fish (pollock, haddock, hake, cod or similar),
  cut in 2cm chunks
3 tbsp plain flour
3 eggs, separated
8 Krisprolls, finely crushed

Heat the oil and the tablespoon of butter in a frying pan and sweat the leek and onion for 8-10 minutes until soft and translucent, then remove from the heat. Add the crème fraîche, milk, nutmeg and allspice berries to the pan and season with a generous pinch of salt and white pepper. Gently bring to a simmer and add the fish. Cover the pan (with its lid or a 'cartouche' – a circle of greaseproof paper cut to the same size as your frying pan) and poach gently over a low heat for 2 minutes.

While the fish is poaching, preheat the oven to 200°C/180°C fan/gas mark 6. Melt the 25g of butter in a small-medium saucepan, stir in the flour and heat together for 1-2 minutes until a pale biscuit colour. Remove from the heat and drain the fish-poaching milk in to this pan through a fine sieve, stirring as you add the hot liquid to create a creamy sauce. Place this saucepan back on the heat and set the drained fish, leek and onion aside in a bowl or on a plate (it's worth removing the allspice berries at this stage if you can spot them).

Whisk the sauce vigorously while it bubbles and thickens over the heat for a couple of minutes until the sauce is lump-free and has a dropping consistency (i.e. it is thick enough not to slide straight off a spoon, but not so thick that it sticks). Season well, as the flavour will be diluted when you add the beaten egg whites.

Remove the sauce from the heat, add the egg yolks and blend through so the sauce looks glossy and smooth. Whisk the egg whites to stiff peaks in a large bowl. Stir the cooked fish and vegetables in to the sauce in stages, then fold in the egg whites until everything is evenly mixed. Gently pour in to a medium-large ceramic or metal roasting tin. Sprinkle the surface with the crushed Krisprolls and dot with a few nuggets of butter.

Bake for 20-25 minutes on the upper-middle shelf of the oven. If the topping still looks a bit pale after that time, simply blast under the grill for a minute to really crisp and colour it up. Serve warm with seasonal greens or a fresh salad.

✳ Traditionally, cooked macaroni is also baked in this pie, which made it a particular favourite of my grandfather's, who loved macaroni in everything. Simply boil 75-100g macaroni or other pasta in salted water until al dente, drain and then add it to the mix when folding in the fish. It might sound odd but the combination of creamy fish pie and the squidgy texture of the macaroni really works…

Roasted cauliflower, anchovy and crème fraîche bake

I've said it before, I'll say it again: I love Abba *anchovies. They are true nostalgia food for me, and are delicious – whether spread on buttered toast soldiers for dipping in soft-boiled eggs or used in classic Scandi dishes like Jansson's Temptation. Where Mediterranean anchovies are dried and salted before being preserved in olive oil, the Scandinavian anchovies (technically sprats) are cured in an aromatic sweet-salt brine. Here, they lift this roasted cauliflower bake to become something much more than the sum of its parts. I like the tang that crème fraîche gives to this dish, but if you prefer a creamier version, use 50:50 crème fraîche and double cream. Crispy Japanese panko breadcrumbs make the perfect topping for this dish, but if you can't get hold of any, use crushed Swedish Krisprolls or normal breadcrumbs instead.*

SERVES 2-3 AT LUNCH OR 4 AS A SIDE DISH

40g butter, plus 1 tbsp for sautéing and more to finish
1 large cauliflower, chopped in small chunks
1 onion, finely sliced
1 tbsp vegetable oil
500g crème fraîche
1 small tin *Abba* anchovies
handful panko (Japanese breadcrumbs) or crushed Krisprolls
2-3 allspice berries, finely ground or crushed

Preheat the oven to 220°C/200°C fan/gas mark 7. Melt the butter in a large pan, toss the cauliflower in it until well coated and season with salt and pepper. Spread the cauliflower on a baking sheet and roast for 10 minutes until it starts to look golden brown. Toss it around a little to ensure that it browns evenly, then leave to cook for a further 5-10 minutes. In the meantime, sauté the onion in the vegetable oil and a tablespoon of butter until soft and translucent.

Remove the roasted cauliflower from the oven. Heat the crème fraîche in a saucepan until simmering. Put the cauliflower in a 20cm x 30cm (or thereabouts) ceramic roasting dish, sprinkle the anchovies and onion over it and then pour the hot crème fraîche over the top. Taste for seasoning – you may need to stir in a pinch or two of salt. Finally, sprinkle the panko or Krisproll crumbs on top along with the ground allspice and a few small nuggets of cold butter.

Bake for 20 minutes or so until the sauce is bubbling and the topping is golden brown and crispy. Remove from the oven and allow to cool for a few minutes before tucking in.

VARIATIONS

If you'd like to make this a vegetarian dish simply omit the anchovies and add about 50g grated cheese (*Västerbotten*, Cheddar, Lancashire or Gorwydd Caerphilly – or all of the above!) for a cheesy cauliflower bake.

Try mixing mushrooms or other vegetables with the cauliflower – simply sauté and season with salt, pepper and maybe a little garlic before adding to the cauliflower mixture.

For bacon lovers, a handful of sautéed bacon bits sprinkled over the cauliflower instead of anchovies goes down a treat.

Crispy baked salmon

This is one of my favourite ways to bake salmon and is a hybrid of several recipes I've tried over the years. All the sweet, sour, spicy, salty and savoury umami flavours of the crisp crust combine to make a fabulous foil for the rich oily salmon. Japanese panko breadcrumbs are, in my humble opinion, the best breadcrumbs on the planet, but if you can't get hold of them, use crushed Swedish Krisprolls or normal breadcrumbs instead. As for which mustard you use for the sauce – English if you like it strong, Dijon if you don't!

SERVES 6

butter
6 large salmon fillets
3 tbsp English or Dijon mustard
3 tbsp horseradish sauce, plus more to glaze
3 *Abba* anchovy fillets, finely chopped
zest and juice of 2 lemons
2 tsp English mustard powder
2 tsp demerara sugar
1 tsp finely crushed allspice
75g panko (Japanese breadcrumbs)
crème fraîche to serve

Butter a large roasting tin and place the salmon fillets in it, taking care to space them a few centimetres apart.

Mix the mustard, horseradish, anchovies, zest and juice of one lemon, mustard powder, demerara sugar and allspice together in a medium bowl to form a thick paste. Tip in the panko breadcrumbs and quickly toss them in this mixture. You don't want the panko getting soggy but make sure to coat the breadcrumbs with as much of the seasoning as possible.

Preheat the oven to 200°C/180°C fan/gas mark 6. Using a pastry brush, glaze each salmon fillet with a thin layer of horseradish. Season with salt and pepper before grating the zest of the second lemon over the salmon. Then divide the breadcrumb mixture between the fillets, gently covering each one with a good layer (I find it easiest to use my hands to do this).

Put the roasting tin on the middle shelf of the oven and bake for 15-20 minutes until the salmon looks opaque and the breadcrumbs look golden and crispy. If the salmon is fully cooked but the topping is still a little underdone, just pop the tin under a medium grill for a couple of minutes but be careful not to burn the topping – it's easily done!

Serve immediately with a dollop of crème fraîche, a good spritz of lemon juice and some steamed seasonal greens, and maybe some roasted beetroot and herby new potatoes too.

Karelian pies

This recipe is from my Finnish friend Eleonoora. The little pastries are made with rye flour for extra flavour and robustness, and the creamy rice filling is utterly more-ish. The butter is essential so don't even think about leaving it out. After all, Karelian pies are only truly Karelian if there are lashings of butter involved...

MAKES 8-10

Rice
75g pudding rice
30g butter
500ml milk

Pastry
100g rye flour
50g refined spelt
 (or plain) flour
½ tsp salt
15g butter, melted,
 plus 50g for glazing

Egg butter
1 medium egg,
 hardboiled
 and peeled
25g butter, softened

Put the rice in a saucepan with 150ml water, bring to the boil and cook for 5 minutes. Add the butter and milk, reduce to a low simmer and cook for a further 30-45 minutes until the rice is soft and thick. Season with salt and cool slightly before assembling the pies.

While the rice is cooking, blitz the pastry ingredients in a blender or food processor (or mix together in a large bowl with a knife or your hands) until you have a firm but pliable dough. Shape in to a thick sausage shape (about 5cm in diameter) and cover with clingfilm and put in the fridge to chill for at least 30 minutes.

After 30 minutes of chilling, remove the pastry from the fridge and slice in to 8-10 discs. Roll the discs out on a lightly floured surface until each one is only a couple of millimetres thick – basically as thin as you can, so it's crisp when baked.

Preheat the oven to 200°C/180°C fan/gas mark 6 and line a large baking tray with baking parchment. Place the discs on the baking tray and lightly glaze them with melted butter. Flip them over so the buttered side faces downwards. Place a dollop of cooked rice in the middle of each pastry round, leaving a couple of centimetres of pastry around the edge. Then fold up the edges around the cooked rice, pinching the pastry as you fold it so the edges have a crimped effect. Leave the centre of rice filling uncovered. Brush again with the rest of the melted butter and bake in the oven for 10-15 minutes until the pastry feels crisp and looks brown. While the pies are baking, mash the hardboiled egg with the softened butter.

Serve the pies warm and eat with a teaspoon of egg butter smeared on top.

✳ It's not strictly Finnish but if you want to make a sweet version of these pies, add some vanilla extract and a couple of spoonfuls of sugar to the rice, omit the egg butter and serve instead with a dusting of cinnamon.

Pastries, sweet buns and muffins

What kind of Scandinavian baking

book would this be, if there weren't any Danish pastry recipes?
Danish pastry is thought to stem originally from Vienna, and it is known
across Scandinavia as *wienerbrød* (Viennese bread) in recognition of
those Austrian roots. The enriched yeast dough contains milk, egg and –
famously – a lot of butter. A little bit of technique and patience is required,
but the effort is truly worth it for an authentic Danish pastry experience,
so why not try your hand at making *frøsnapper*, sesame and poppy seed twists
with a buttery almond middle, custard-filled *spandauer* or little jam-centred
pinwheel stars for an impressive brunch or coffee morning?

Sweet buns are a real favourite of mine. They remind me of my
Norwegian grandmother, who taught me how to make *skoleboller* (school
buns), cardamom dough filled with home-made vanilla custard and
sprinkled with desiccated coconut… sheer heaven in a bun. And then there
are spiced blueberry buns, Santa Lucia sour cherry and saffron buns,
cardamom almond twists, stickily delicious cinnamon bun-cake and more
– all perfect for elevenses, afternoon tea or just a little snackerel when you
fancy something sweet.

Muffins are a more recent addition to the Scandinavian baking pantheon
and I adore baking them, not least because they're super quick to make,
so there are mere minutes from mixing everything together to scoffing
them fresh from the oven. The secret is to pack in lots of flavour – summery
greengage and elderflower, zesty pink grapefruit, luscious blueberry and
raspberry or wickedly good *Daim* chocolate – the only question is which
one to try first!

Mini cardamom buns with almond custard
Skoleboller — Norwegian custard
 and coconut buns
Cardamom almond twists
Cinnamon bun-cake
Kardemommesnurrer —
 cardamom swirl bun-pops
Scandilicious Chelsea buns
Santa Lucia sour cherry and saffron buns
Spiced blueberry buns
Daim chocolate muffins
Greengage and elderflower muffins
Pink grapefruit marmalade muffins
Queen Maud muffins
Wienerbrød — Danish pastry
Spandauer — custard-filled Danish pastries
Frøsnapper — sesame and poppy Danish twists
Jam star Danish pastries
Almond *kringle* wreath
Tebirkes — poppy seed Danish pastries

Mini cardamom buns with almond custard

Filled cardamom buns are traditionally eaten in Norway, Sweden and Denmark on Shrove Tuesday, but I love them any time of the year. These are a bite-sized version of the Scandi favourite and contain almond custard rather than the usual lightly whipped vanilla cream and marzipan. You can use ready-made fresh custard if you are time-pressed, but I find that home-made just tastes so much better. The baked but uncut, unfilled buns can be stored for a day or two in an airtight container before filling, or you can freeze them to eat at a later date. I recommend making the dough the night before baking as the overnight ferment really improves flavour and texture, and I make the custard the day before too, but you can do it all on the same day if that's easier – allow 30 minutes or so in a warm place for the first proving (rather than overnight) and do remember to double the quantity of yeast to compensate for the shorter proving time.

MAKES 24

Dough

325ml whole milk
50g butter
500g refined spelt (or plain) flour
75g caster sugar
1½ tsp ground cardamom
2 tsp fine sea salt
15g fresh yeast or 7g fast action
  dried yeast

Filling

1 batch *skoleboller* custard (page 96) or
  500ml ready-made fresh custard
50g whole almonds, roughly crushed

To finish

1 medium egg, beaten
icing sugar to dust

Scald the milk by heating it in a small pan with the butter until it is almost boiling and then allow it to cool while you assemble the other ingredients. Scalding the milk makes the finished buns softer.

Sift the flour, sugar, cardamom and salt together in to a large bowl. If using fresh yeast, cream it with a teaspoon of sugar in a small bowl and once it is liquid (after about 30 seconds), add to the dry ingredients.

Make a well in the middle of the dry ingredients and add the scalded milk, which should be warm rather than hot to the touch, as otherwise you risk killing the yeast. Stir everything together until the mixture comes off the sides of the bowl and looks – for want of a better word – doughy. Place the dough in a lightly oiled plastic bag and leave overnight to cold ferment in the fridge. Be aware that the carbon dioxide gas from fermentation will expand the bag so make sure you leave plenty of space around the dough.

Follow the *skoleboller* custard recipe (page 96) and after you have stirred in the vanilla extract, stir in the crushed almonds (or stir the almonds in to the ready-made custard, if using). Then pour in to a bowl and cover with clingfilm so that it sits directly on the surface of the custard, to stop a skin developing. Allow to cool completely before refrigerating until needed.

When you are ready to bake, remove the dough from the fridge and allow to come to room temperature. Lightly oil two baking sheets. Divide the dough in two and keep one half

covered with lightly oiled clingfilm while you divide the other half in 12 equal-sized pieces (either by weighing or just judge it by eye) and then roll them in to little round buns. Repeat with other half of the dough, cover the buns again and set aside to prove in a warm place for 15-20 minutes until they don't spring back – i.e. if you poke one lightly with your little finger, the indentation stays put. Lightly glaze each bun with a little beaten egg.

Preheat the oven to 200°C/180°C fan/gas mark 6. Splash a little water in the bottom of the oven to create steam to help them to rise. Bake on the upper middle shelf for 10-15 minutes, turning the heat down to 180°C/160°C fan/gas mark 4 if the buns start to take on too much colour.

The cooked buns should look golden brown and sound hollow when you tap them. Allow to cool on a wire rack. When you're ready to fill the buns, simply halve and dollop a spoonful of almond custard on the bottom half, then cover with the top half and dust with icing sugar. Eat with obvious enjoyment, and the great excuse that these don't keep long…

Skoleboller – Norwegian custard and coconut buns

Skoleboller, or school buns, remind me of my childhood. In Norway and Sweden these cardamom buns are filled with vivid yellow custard and topped with icing and coconut. I find them sweet enough without icing, but feel free to drizzle with a sugar glaze before dusting with coconut. I sprinkle the coconut on before baking for a toasted topping, but you can add it halfway through if you prefer. You can use 500ml ready-made fresh custard to fill them if you're time-pressed, but why not make your own with this simple recipe (any left over makes a a fantastic late-night snack). I recommend making the dough the night before baking as the overnight ferment really improves flavour and texture, and I make the custard the day before too, but you can do it all on the same day if that's easier – allow 30 minutes or so in a warm place for the first proving (rather than overnight) and do remember to double the quantity of yeast to compensate for the shorter proving time.

MAKES 16

Dough
325ml whole milk
50g butter
500g refined spelt (or plain) flour
75g caster sugar
1½ tsp ground cardamom
2 tsp fine sea salt
15g fresh yeast or 7g fast action dried yeast
1 medium egg, beaten

Filling
4 medium egg yolks
40g cornflour
500ml whole milk
75g caster sugar
¼ tsp fine sea salt
1 tsp vanilla extract

To finish
1 medium egg, beaten
unsweetened desiccated coconut

Scald the milk by heating it in a small pan with the butter until it is almost boiling and then allow it to cool while you assemble the other ingredients. Scalding the milk makes the finished buns softer.

Sift the flour, sugar, cardamom and salt together in to a large bowl. If using fresh yeast, cream it with a teaspoon of sugar in a small bowl and once it is liquid (after about 30 seconds), add to the dry ingredients.

Make a well in the middle of the dry ingredients, add the beaten egg and then the milk-butter mixture, which should be warm rather than hot to the touch, as otherwise you risk killing the yeast. Stir everything together until the mixture comes off the sides of the bowl and looks – for want of a better word – doughy. Place the dough in a lightly oiled plastic bag and leave overnight to cold ferment in the fridge. Be aware that the carbon dioxide gas from fermentation will expand the bag, so make sure you leave plenty of space around the dough.

Put the egg yolks and cornflour in a bowl and whisk together so the cornflour is distributed evenly. In a saucepan bring the milk and sugar to a simmer and then remove from the heat. Pour a third of the hot sweetened milk on to the egg yolks and stir through to temper the yolks. Pour this mixture back in to the saucepan containing the rest of the sweetened milk, add the salt and bring to a gentle boil while stirring constantly (boiling it helps it to thicken but you need to keep stirring to avoid getting lumpy custard). Remove from the heat and sieve if any lumps have appeared despite your best efforts. Add the vanilla extract and stir through. Pour in to a bowl and cover with clingfilm so that it sits directly on the surface of the custard, to stop a skin developing. Allow to cool completely before refrigerating until needed.

When you are ready to bake, remove the dough from the fridge and allow to come to room temperature. Lightly oil two baking sheets. Divide the dough in two and keep one half covered with lightly oiled clingfilm while you divide the other half in eight equal-sized pieces (either by weighing or just judge it by eye) and then roll them in to little round buns. Repeat with other half of the dough, cover the buns again and set aside to prove in a warm place for 15-20 minutes until they don't spring back – i.e. if you poke one lightly with your little finger, the indentation stays put.

Preheat the oven to 200°C/180°C fan/gas mark 6. Dip a pastry brush handle in the beaten egg and use to make a hollow in the top of each bun, pressing about two-thirds of the way down in to the dough. The deeper and wider the hollow you make, the more custard you'll be able to fit in!

Spoon vanilla custard in to the hollow on each bun, brush the bun's surface with beaten egg and sprinkle coconut over the top. Splash a little water in the bottom of the oven to create steam to help them rise. Bake on the upper middle shelf for 10-15 minutes, turning the heat down to 180°C/160°C fan/gas mark 4 if the buns start to take on too much colour.

The cooked buns should look golden brown and sound hollow when you tap them on the base. Allow to cool on a wire rack before eating. These buns freeze well – simply defrost at room temperature overnight to enjoy the following day (don't try to reheat them or the custard will split).

Cardamom almond twists

*We adore almonds and marzipan in Scandinavia and these twists encompass the best of Scandi baking for me –
twisted knot-shaped cardamom buns with a sweet marzipan-like filling and a crunchy sprinkling of almonds
on top. Traditional almond remonce filling can be overly sweet, so I've reduced the sugar and added more
almonds, along with a non-traditional ingredient – crème fraîche – to bind it all together and balance the flavours.
You can add two teaspoonfuls of cinnamon to the filling too if, like me, you are partial to a bit of spice.
I recommend making the dough the night before baking as the overnight ferment really improves flavour and texture,
but you can do it all on the same day if that's easier – allow 30 minutes or so in a warm place for the first proving
(rather than overnight) and do remember to double the quantity of yeast to compensate for the shorter proving time.*

Dough

325ml whole milk
50g butter
500g refined spelt
  (or plain) flour
75g caster sugar
1½ tsp ground cardamom
2 tsp fine sea salt
15g fresh yeast or 7g
  fast action dried yeast
1 medium egg, beaten

Filling

75g butter, softened
50g ground almonds
50g *mandelmasse*
  (50% almond paste)
  or marzipan
50g caster sugar
3 tbsp crème fraîche
1 tsp vanilla extract
¼ tsp fine sea salt

To finish

1 medium egg, beaten
flaked almonds

Scald the milk by heating it with the butter in a small pan with the butter until it is almost boiling and then allow it to cool while you assemble the other ingredients. Scalding the milk makes the finished buns softer.

Sift the flour, sugar, cardamom and salt together in to a large bowl. If using fresh yeast, cream it with a teaspoon of sugar in a small bowl and once it is liquid (after about 30 seconds), add to the dry ingredients.

Make a well in the middle of the dry ingredients, add the beaten egg and then the milk-butter mixture, which should be warm rather than hot to the touch, as otherwise you risk killing the yeast. Stir everything together until the mixture comes off the sides of the bowl and looks – for want of a better word – doughy. Place the dough in a lightly oiled plastic bag and leave overnight to cold ferment in the fridge. Be aware that the carbon dioxide gas from fermentation will expand the bag so make sure you leave plenty of space around the dough.

When you are ready to bake, remove the dough from the fridge and allow to come to room temperature for 30 minutes or so. In the meantime, blitz the filling ingredients together in a food processor or cream together in a medium bowl with a wooden spoon until you have a sticky almondy paste.

Roll out the dough on a lightly floured surface until it forms a large rectangle approximately 30cm x 50cm. Using a spatula, spread the almond filling over half of the pastry lengthways, so that one side (roughly 15cm x 50cm) is smoothly covered. Fold the other half of the dough on top of the filling-covered section, pressing gently around the edges and dabbing them with a bit of water to seal in the almond filling.

Use a sharp knife to slice the dough in to 16 or 20 strips (depending upon how big you want to make the buns). Pick up a strip of dough and twist the ends in opposite directions two or three times and then coil the strip in on itself, tucking the ends underneath and sealing them in place with a dab of water. Once you have twisted all the strips, place them on a lined baking sheet, cover with lightly oiled clingfilm and leave to prove in a warm place for 10-15 minutes until the dough no longer springs back when prodded gently with your little finger.

Preheat the oven to 200°C/180°C fan/gas mark 6. Glaze the twists with beaten egg and scatter flaked almonds over them. Bake on the middle shelf of the oven for 15 minutes, checking after 10 minutes to see that they aren't taking on too much colour or singeing. If you find that they are getting too dark, lower the temperature by 20°C or so until they are cooked through and sound hollow when you tap them on the base.

Allow to cool on a wire rack before eating.

Cinnamon bun-cake

Cinnamon buns are quintessentially Scandinavian, and you will find subtle variations on this tasty treat across Norway, Sweden, Denmark and Finland. This cinnamon bun-cake looks very festive and inviting – it is perfect to share at brunch or afternoon tea.

SERVES 7

Dough

225ml whole milk
75g butter
300g refined spelt
  (or plain) flour
125g wholemeal spelt
  (or wheat) flour
70g caster sugar
1 tsp ground cardamom
½ tsp fine sea salt
20g fresh yeast or 10g
  fast action dried yeast
1 medium egg, beaten

Filling

75g butter, softened
50g caster sugar
2 tsp cinnamon
½ tsp vanilla salt

To finish

1 medium egg, beaten
demerara or natural
  sugar crystals

Scald the milk by heating it in a small pan with the butter until it is almost boiling and then allow it to cool while you assemble the other ingredients. Scalding the milk makes the finished buns softer.

Sift all the dry ingredients together in to a large bowl, sprinkle the dried yeast in and stir through. If using fresh yeast, cream it with a teaspoon of sugar in a small bowl and once it is liquid (after about 30 seconds), add to the dry ingredients.

Make a well in the middle of the dry ingredients, add the beaten egg and then the milk-butter mixture, which should be warm rather than hot to the touch, as otherwise you risk killing the yeast. Stir everything together until the mixture comes off the sides of the bowl and looks – for want of a better word – doughy (it'll be a soft and slightly wet dough). Place the dough in a lightly oiled plastic bag or cover the bowl with lightly oiled clingfilm, and leave it to rise in a warm place for 30 minutes.

Make the filling by creaming the butter, sugar, cinnamon and vanilla salt together in a medium-sized bowl. Butter a 23cm diameter round cake tin with sides at least 5cm high.

Use a rolling pin to roll out the dough on a lightly floured surface until it forms a rectangle of about 35cm x 25cm. Spread the filling evenly over the dough, starting from the middle and working outwards. If the buttery mix is a little cold, you can use your hands to spread it, as the heat helps to smooth the butter out (and it's immensely satisfying getting your hands all sticky). Then roll the dough in to a wide cylinder, rolling from one of the longer edges of the rectangle, so it looks like an uncooked swiss roll.

Using a sharp non-serrated knife, cut the cylinder in to seven slices, with one slice slightly smaller than the rest. Place the smallest slice in the middle of the cake tin and then evenly space the remaining six around the middle one. Cover the buns and leave to rise again in a warm place for 20-30 minutes until they have doubled in size. You can test to see if they've proved enough by gently poking one bun with your little finger – the indentation should stay put.

Preheat the oven to 200°C/180°C fan/gas mark 6. Glaze the risen buns with beaten egg and sprinkle demerara or natural sugar crystals over the top. Splash a little water in the bottom of the oven to create steam to help the bun-cake to rise. Bake on the middle shelf of the oven for 20-25 minutes or until it sounds hollow when tapped on the base and looks golden brown.

Allow to cool on a wire rack. This will last for a couple of days and freezes well.

Kardemommesnurrer – cardamom swirl bun-pops

These swirly bun lollipops look pretty, taste great and are a doddle to make, so this is a perfect rainy day baking recipe for bored children (or grown-ups)! Cardamom can be quite an adult flavour, so if you're catering for kids who aren't cardamom fans, try leaving it out and adding a few tablespoons of melted chocolate or chocolate-hazelnut spread to the butter mixture or use 125g fruity jam instead to transform these in to chocolate or fruit swirl pops. Whatever the filling, they're dangerously tasty…

MAKES 25-30

Dough
225ml whole milk
75g butter
300g refined spelt
  (or plain) flour
125g wholemeal spelt
  (or wheat) flour
70g caster sugar
1 tsp ground cardamom
½ tsp cinnamon
½ tsp fine sea salt
20g fresh yeast or 10g
  fast action dried yeast
1 medium egg, beaten

Filling
75g butter, softened
50g caster sugar
2 tsp ground cardamom
½ tsp vanilla salt

To finish
1 medium egg, beaten
demerara or
  natural sugar crystals

Soak 25-30 wooden lolly sticks, each roughly 10cm long, in cold water.

Scald the milk by heating it in a small pan with the butter until it is almost boiling and then allow it to cool while you assemble the other ingredients. Scalding the milk makes the finished bun-pops softer.

Sift all the dry ingredients together in to a large bowl, sprinkle the dried yeast in and stir through. If using fresh yeast, cream it with a teaspoon of sugar in a small bowl and once it is liquid (after about 30 seconds), add to the dry ingredients.

Make a well in the middle of the dry ingredients, add the beaten egg and then the milk-butter mixture, which should be warm rather than hot to the touch, as otherwise you risk killing the yeast. Stir everything together until the mixture comes off the sides of the bowl and looks – for want of a better word – doughy (it'll be a soft and slightly wet dough). Place the dough in a lightly oiled plastic bag or cover the bowl with lightly oiled clingfilm, and leave it to rise in a warm place for 30 minutes.

While the dough is proving, make the filling by creaming the butter, sugar, cardamom and vanilla salt together. Oil two large baking sheets.

Divide the dough in half (either by weighing or judging by eye) and roll out one piece on a lightly floured surface until it forms a rectangle about 25cm x 15cm (keep the other half of the dough covered with a damp teatowel or lightly oiled clingfilm while you do this so it doesn't dry out). Spread half the filling evenly over the rectangle, starting from the middle and working outwards. If the buttery mix is a little cold, you can use your hands to spread it, as the heat helps to smooth the butter out (and it's immensely satisfying getting your hands all sticky!) Then, rolling from one of the longer edges of the rectangle, roll the dough in to a long cylinder so it looks like an uncooked swiss roll, then seal the join at the end with a little water.

Use a sharp non-serrated knife to cut the log in to 12-15 even slices and lay them flat. Starting at the join in the dough, push a wooden stick in from the outer edge of each slice until it is about halfway through the swirl. Make sure that the sticks are secure and then place the bun-pops on one of the baking sheets, cover with oiled clingfilm and leave to rise in a warm place for 20-30 minutes until they have doubled in size and an indentation stays put if you gently prod the dough with your little finger. Repeat the rolling, filling, slicing and lollypopping process with the other half of the dough while the first batch of bun-pops is proving, and then leave the second batch to prove on the other baking sheet.

Preheat the oven to 200°C/180°C fan/gas mark 6. Glaze the first batch of bun-pops with beaten egg, sprinkle with demerara or natural sugar crystals and then bake on the middle shelf of the oven for 12-15 minutes until they are golden brown and sound hollow when you tap them on the base. Leave to cool on a wire rack while you bake the second batch (once they've finished proving).

Stand the bun-pops upright in a jar,
jug, glass or mug to serve.

Scandilicious Chelsea buns

This is an enriched spelt version of a traditional Chelsea bun, made with fruit soaked in Lady Grey tea and a lovely marmalade glaze inspired by top baker Dan Lepard. I find that the citrus-flavoured Lady Grey and the marmalade glaze make perfect partners, but if you prefer you could use a different type of tea, or even brandy, sherry or whisky, to soak the fruit. Similarly, feel free to omit the lemon zest at the end or replace it with orange zest if you prefer. Do note that if you are going to be leaving the dough to ferment overnight in the fridge, you only need to use half the quantity of yeast specified below.

MAKES 15-20

Dough
340ml whole milk
75g butter
550g refined spelt (or plain) flour
60g golden caster sugar
1½ tsp cinnamon
½ tsp mixed spice
1½ tsp fine sea salt
20g fresh yeast or 10g fast action dried yeast
2 medium eggs, beaten

Filling
80g currants
80g sultanas
1 large mug (at least 250ml) strong Lady Grey tea
150g butter
100g light brown muscovado sugar
1 tsp vanilla salt
1½ tsp cinnamon
½ tsp mixed spice
demerara sugar or natural sugar crystals for sprinkling (optional)

Glaze
1 jar (284g) marmalade
40g butter
zest of 1 lemon (and juice, optional)

Scald the milk by heating it in a small pan with the butter until it is almost boiling and then allow it to cool while you assemble the other ingredients. Scalding the milk makes the finished buns softer.

Sift all the dry ingredients together in to a large bowl, sprinkle the dried yeast in and stir through. If using fresh yeast, cream it with a teaspoon of sugar in a small bowl and once it is liquid (after about 30 seconds), add to the dry ingredients.

Make a well in the middle of the dry ingredients, add the beaten eggs and then the milk-butter mixture, which should be warm rather than hot to the touch, as otherwise you risk killing the yeast. Stir everything together using a large metal spoon for 5 minutes or so until the mixture comes together.

Cover the dough with lightly oiled clingfilm and set aside in a warm place to rise for an hour or so until it has doubled in size. Alternatively put it in a lightly oiled plastic bag and leave it in the fridge overnight to bubble and ferment for a slower maturation and more complex flavour. Be aware that the carbon dioxide gas from fermentation will expand the bag so make sure you leave plenty of space around the dough. Put the currants, sultanas and tea in a small bowl, cover and leave to soak while the dough is proving (i.e. an hour or overnight), then drain.

If the dough proved in the fridge overnight, leave it to come back to room temperature for 30 minutes or so before knocking back. Knead for one minute, then roll it out on a lightly floured surface to make a rectangle roughly 40cm x 25cm.

Cream together the butter, sugar, vanilla salt and spices in a medium bowl before spreading in an even layer across dough, then scatter the soaked fruit evenly over the top. Roll the dough up like a swiss roll using a dough scraper or palette knife to lift it as you go. Dab water along the dough edge where it joins the roll and gently press to seal, then turn the roll over so the join seam is underneath.

Line a large baking tray with baking parchment. Use a sharp knife to slice the rolled dough, making each slice about 2.5cm wide. Place the dough slices flat on the lined tray, leaving about 5cm between them. Cover with lightly oiled cling film and set aside to prove in a warm place for 30 minutes or so until they have puffed up and doubled in size. Test by pressing the dough gently with a finger – the impression made shouldn't spring back.

Preheat the oven to 200°C/180°C fan/gas mark 6. Sprinkle the proved buns with demerara sugar or sugar crystals (if using) and bake on the upper middle shelf of the oven for 5 minutes before reducing the temperature to 180°C/160°C fan/gas mark 4 for a further 20 minutes or so until the buns look golden brown and sound hollow when you tap on the base.

Leave the buns to cool on a wire rack while you warm the marmalade, butter and a splash of water or lemon juice in a small saucepan. Using a pastry brush, generously glaze the buns with the marmalade mixture and sprinkle the lemon zest on top. Eat while the buns are warm and serve (of course) with a steaming cup of Lady Grey tea.

Santa Lucia sour cherry and saffron buns

Every year in Scandinavia on December 13th, the advent festival of Santa Lucia is celebrated with candles, singing and lussekatter *– saffron-scented S-shaped buns, stuffed with currants or raisins – served with hot chocolate for children and* gløgg *(mulled wine) for adults. The name* lussekatter *is thought to refer to Lucifer's cats, and these yellow buns were originally intended to ward off the devil! I have tweaked the traditional recipe, adding cardamom and substituting dried sour cherries for the usual currants or raisins. You can use any dried fruit, apricots, dates, prunes or a mixture to suit your taste, but I think the combination of saffron, cardamom and sour cherry is – forgive the pun – devilishly good.*

MAKES 12

325ml whole milk	1 tsp ground cardamom
a few saffron threads	4 tbsp caster sugar
15g fresh yeast or 7g fast action dried yeast	1 tsp fine sea salt
50g butter	1 medium egg, beaten, plus more
350g refined spelt (or plain) flour	to glaze
150g wholemeal spelt flour	24-48 dried sour cherries

Heat the milk with the saffron strands in a small pan. Allow to cool until lukewarm and then pour in to a bowl and dissolve the yeast in it. Melt the butter separately, allow to cool slightly and then stir through the milk mixture. Sift the flours, cardamom, sugar and salt together in a large bowl, stir in the milk mixture and a beaten egg, and continue to stir until you have a sticky dough.

Turn the dough on to a floured surface and knead for 5 minutes until it starts to feel smooth and elastic (it is quite a wet dough so you may want to use a dough scraper during the early stages). Put the dough back in the mixing bowl, cover with a damp tea towel or lightly oiled clingfilm and leave in a warm place to rise for about 1-1½ hours until it has doubled in size.

Tip the dough out on a floured surface and punch once or twice to knock it back. Knead and shape in to a log and then slice in to 12 pieces of roughly equal size (judging by eye or by weighing). Roll each piece in to a sausage and then shape like an S. Place the S-shaped buns on parchment paper, cover with a damp tea towel or lightly oiled clingfilm and leave in a warm place for 20-30 minutes to prove and double in size again.

Preheat the oven to 200°C/180°C fan/gas mark 6 while the buns are proving. Once they have risen, push a dried sour cherry or two in to the crease of the bends in the S-shaped bun, pressing them well in to the dough so they don't pop up during baking! Lightly glaze each bun with a little beaten egg and bake on the upper shelf of the oven for 20 minutes or so, by which time they should look golden yellow and sound hollow when you tap them on the base.

Serve warm with cold milk, hot chocolate, or *gløgg* (mulled wine).

Spiced blueberry buns

These buns were inspired by my love of Eccles cakes and are delicious – at once buttery, spicy, fruity and sweet. Bursting with flavour, the soft cardamom-scented dough gives way to a rich cinnamon-blueberry filling. No surprise, then, that everyone I know who has tried them devours them in seconds!

MAKES 12-14

Dough

225ml whole milk
75g butter
300g refined spelt
  (or plain) flour
125g wholemeal spelt (or
wheat) flour
70g caster sugar
1 tsp ground cardamom
½ tsp fine sea salt
20g fresh yeast or 10g
  fast action dried yeast
1 medium egg, beaten

Filling

75g butter, softened
75g caster sugar
2 tsp cinnamon
300g fresh or frozen
  blueberries

To finish

1 medium egg white, beaten
demerara sugar or
  caster sugar

Scald the milk by heating it in a small pan with the butter until it is almost boiling and then allow it to cool while you assemble the other ingredients. Scalding the milk makes the finished buns softer.

Sift all the dry ingredients together in to a large bowl, sprinkle the dried yeast in and stir through. If using fresh yeast, cream it with a teaspoon of sugar in a small bowl and once it is liquid (after about 30 seconds), add to the dry ingredients.

Make a well in the middle of the dry ingredients, add the beaten egg and then the milk-butter mixture, which should be warm rather than hot to the touch, as otherwise you risk killing the yeast. Stir everything together until the mixture comes off the sides of the bowl and looks – for want of a better word – doughy (it'll be a soft and slightly wet dough). Place the dough in a lightly oiled plastic bag or cover the bowl with lightly oiled clingfilm, and leave it to rise in a warm place for 30 minutes.

While the dough is proving, make the filling by creaming the butter, sugar and cinnamon together.

Divide the dough in to 12 roughly equal pieces (either by weighing or judging by eye) and flatten them slightly so they resemble fat pancakes. Spread some cinnamon butter on each one and sprinkle with a tablespoon or so of blueberries.
Dab a little water around the edges of the dough and then carefully gather up and pinch together so that the blueberries and filling are sealed in a dough parcel. Turn the parcels over and place join-side down on a floured baking tray. Cover with oiled clingfilm and leave to rise in a warm place for 20-30 minutes until they have doubled in size. You can test the buns by gently poking with your little finger – the indentation should stay put.

Preheat the oven to 200°C/180°C fan/gas mark 6. Glaze the proved buns with beaten egg white and sprinkle sugar over the tops. Splash a little water in the bottom of the oven to create steam to help the buns to rise. Bake on the middle shelf of the oven for 12-15 minutes.

Allow the buns to cool on a wire rack before eating, as the filling will be very hot straight out of the oven. They will last for several days and freeze well – simply reheat at 150°C/130°C fan/gas mark 2 for 10-15 minutes and they're like freshly baked buns all over again!

Daim chocolate muffins

These chocolate muffins satisfy a sweet tooth without being too sweet, despite the fact that they contain little nuggets of Daim *almond praline and are topped with a rich chocolate* Daim *glaze.*

MAKES 12

3 medium eggs
100g light brown muscovado sugar
200g refined spelt (or plain) flour
3 tbsp cocoa powder
1 tsp baking powder
¼ tsp bicarbonate of soda
¼ tsp fine sea salt
150ml plain yoghurt (or Greek yoghurt)
50ml whole milk
50g butter, melted
1 shot espresso or 2 tbsp strong coffee
150g *Daim* bar, roughly crushed

Glaze

100g dark chocolate
  (70% cocoa solids), broken in
  small pieces
50g butter
75g icing sugar, plus more to taste
1 shot espresso or 2 tbsp strong coffee
1 tsp vanilla extract
100g *Daim* balls or *Daim* bar,
  finely chopped

Line a 12 cup muffin tray (at least 3-4cm deep) with scrunched up squares of parchment paper or muffin cases, and preheat the oven to 220°C/200°C fan/gas mark 7.

Whisk the eggs and brown sugar together in a large bowl until pale and fluffy. Mix the flour, cocoa, raising agents and salt in a bowl and separately mix the yoghurt, milk, melted butter and coffee together in a jug. Carefully stir the dry and wet ingredients in to the egg mixture in stages, alternating a spoonful of each at a time. Once these are evenly mixed in, fold in the crushed *Daim* pieces.

Use an ice cream scoop or teaspoon to scoop the mixture in to each muffin case until it is three-quarters full, then bake on the upper-middle shelf of the oven for 10 minutes before turning the heat down to 190°C/170°C fan/gas mark 5 and baking for a further 5-10 minutes or until the muffins have risen well. If in doubt insert a skewer in to one – when you remove it there should be no uncooked mixture, only a few crumbs. Allow to cool completely on a wire rack before glazing.

Melt the chocolate and butter in a heatproof bowl over a saucepan of barely simmering water, stirring occasionally to help it along, then remove from the heat and allow to cool slightly. Put 75g icing sugar in a medium bowl, make a well in the middle and stir in the coffee and the vanilla extract until all the icing sugar is incorporated in to a sticky icing. Keep stirring as you slowly drizzle in the melted chocolate-butter mixture and then fold in the *Daim* balls or chopped *Daim*, reserving a few balls or shards to decorate. Taste and add more icing sugar if you feel it needs it.

Drizzle the glaze on the muffins and allow to set before topping with the reserved *Daim*. Eat with a big chocolatey smile.

Greengage and elderflower muffins

The inclusion of crème fraîche here helps the muffins to rise and keeps them light and airy. The elderflower flavour is quite subtle so use the highest concentration cordial you can find, as a weakly flavoured one will just result in sweetened greengages – still tasty but you'll lose the magic of the elderflower-greengage combination. If you'd prefer to omit the ground almonds, simply increase the amount of flour by 50g. These muffins also work well with Victoria plums, summer berries, thinly sliced rhubarb (macerated in a little sugar first) or orange and/or lemon zest. Dark chocolate chips would be an excellent addition too...

MAKES 12

12 ripe greengages
40ml elderflower cordial/syrup
3 medium eggs, beaten
150g caster sugar, plus more for sprinkling
200g refined spelt (or plain) flour
50g ground almonds
1½ tsp baking powder
¼ tsp bicarbonate of soda
¼ tsp fine sea salt
200g crème fraîche
50g butter, melted

Line a 12 cup muffin tray (at least 3-4cm deep) with scrunched up squares of parchment paper or muffin cases, and preheat the oven to 220°C/200°C fan/gas mark 7.

Quarter the greengages and remove the stones. Place in a bowl and drizzle the elderflower cordial over them, stirring to ensure they're well coated.

Mix the eggs and sugar together in a medium bowl. Put the flour, ground almonds, raising agents and salt in a large bowl and stir to distribute the raising agents evenly. Make a well in the middle and pour in the egg mixture, the crème fraîche and the melted butter. Stir 4-5 times to mix everything together and then tip in the greengages in their elderflower cordial. Mix 4-5 times more. The trick with muffins is not to overmix the batter, so err on the side of caution and stir up to 12 times altogether but no more (any pockets of flour you come across can be teased out and mixed in using the tip of a sharp knife or a skewer).

Use an ice cream scoop or teaspoon to scoop the mixture in to each muffin case until it is three-quarters full, then sprinkle extra caster sugar on top for a crunchy muffin top.

Bake on the upper-middle shelf of the oven for 10 minutes before turning the heat down to 190°C/170°C fan/gas mark 5 and baking for a further 5-10 minutes or until the muffins have risen well and look pale golden brown. If in doubt insert a skewer in to one – when you remove it there should be no uncooked mixture, only a few crumbs.

Cool on a wire rack. These keep for a day or two in an airtight container, or you can freeze them in foil for a couple of months. Just reheat from frozen at 150°C/130°C fan/gas mark 2 for 15 minutes for fresh muffins on lazy weekend mornings.

Pink grapefruit marmalade muffins

I love pink grapefruit, both as fruit and as juice, and it is a daily ritual in the Johansen household to have half a grapefruit for breakfast. This is an indulgent spin on that breakfast tradition, adapted from an orange marmalade muffin recipe from Fiona Beckett. If you're not such a pink grapefruit fan, simply substitute a different citrus fruit and marmalade. You can choose whether to finish these muffins with a crunchy sugar crust, sprinkled on before baking, or a zesty marmalade glaze, brushed on after baking. You could even scatter oat or spelt flakes on them before baking too, for a little extra wholesome goodness.

MAKES 12

3 medium eggs, beaten

120g caster sugar, plus more
    for sprinkling (optional)

125g pink grapefruit marmalade,
    plus 50g to glaze (optional)

75ml freshly squeezed pink
    grapefruit juice, plus
    2-3 tbsp to glaze (optional)

2 tsp finely grated pink grapefruit
    zest, plus 1 tsp to glaze (optional)

300g refined spelt
    (or plain) flour

50g oat bran

1½ tsp baking powder

¼ tsp bicarbonate of soda

¼ tsp fine sea salt

200g crème fraîche

50g butter, melted

Line a 12 cup muffin tray (at least 3-4cm deep) with scrunched up squares of parchment paper or muffin cases, and preheat the oven to 220°C/200°C fan/gas mark 7.

Mix the eggs and sugar together in a medium bowl. Mix the pink grapefruit marmalade with the grapefruit juice and zest in a separate bowl and stir well. Put the flour, oat bran, raising agents and salt in a large bowl and stir to distribute the raising agents evenly. Make a well in the middle and pour in the egg mixture, the crème fraîche and the melted butter. Stir 4-5 times to mix everything together and then tip in the pink grapefruit mixture. Mix 4-5 times more. The trick with muffins is not to overmix the batter, so err on the side of caution and stir up to 12 times altogether but no more (any pockets of flour you come across can be teased out and mixed in using the tip of a sharp knife or a skewer).

Use an ice cream scoop or teaspoon to scoop the mixture in to each muffin case until it is three-quarters full, then sprinkle extra caster sugar (if using) on top for a crunchy muffin top.

Bake on the upper-middle shelf of the oven for 10 minutes before turning the heat down to 190°C/170°C fan/gas mark 5 and baking for a further 5-10 minutes or until the muffins have risen well and look pale golden brown. If in doubt insert a skewer in to one – when you remove it there should be no uncooked mixture, only a few crumbs.

Cool on a wire rack. To glaze the muffins, dissolve the extra pink grapefruit marmalade with the additional grapefruit juice and zest in a small pan over a low heat, then brush over the cooled muffins.

These keep for a day or two in an airtight container, or you can freeze them in foil for a couple of months. Just reheat from frozen at 150°C/130°C fan/gas mark 2 for 15 minutes for fresh muffins on lazy weekend mornings.

Queen Maud muffins

Blueberry and raspberry jam is known as Queen Maud's jam in Scandinavia. This simple combination is utterly delicious, the tangy raspberries contrasting with the sweet blueberries. Use fresh berries if you have them in season, but if not these turn out just as well using frozen berries – perfect when you need a taste of summer on cold winter mornings.

MAKES 12

3 medium eggs, beaten
150g caster sugar
2 tbsp plain yoghurt
200ml whole milk
150g refined spelt (or plain) flour
100g wholemeal flour
1½ tsp baking powder
¼ tsp bicarbonate of soda
1 tsp cinnamon (optional)
¼ tsp fine sea salt
75g butter, melted
100g blueberries
100g raspberries
spelt or oat flakes to garnish

Line a 12 cup muffin tray (at least 3-4cm deep) with scrunched up squares of parchment paper or muffin cases, and preheat the oven to 220°C/200°C fan/gas mark 7.

Mix the eggs and sugar together in a medium bowl. Stir the yoghurt in to the milk in a small jug. Put the flours, raising agents, cinnamon (if using) and salt in a large bowl and stir to distribute the raising agents evenly. Make a well in the middle and pour in the egg mixture, the yoghurt-milk mixture and the melted butter. Stir 4-5 times to mix everything together and then fold in the berries, working gently but quickly so the berries don't bleed too much in to the mixture. Mix 4-5 times more. The trick with muffins is not to overmix the batter, so err on the side of caution and stir up to 12 times altogether but no more (any pockets of flour you come across can be teased out and mixed in using the tip of a sharp knife or a skewer).

Use an ice cream scoop or teaspoon to scoop the mixture in to each muffin case until it is three-quarters full, then sprinkle the tops with spelt or oat flakes.

Bake on the upper-middle shelf of the oven for 10 minutes before turning the heat down to 190°C/170°C fan/gas mark 5 and baking for a further 5-10 minutes or until the muffins have risen well and look pale golden brown. If in doubt insert a skewer in to one – when you remove it there should be no uncooked mixture, only a few crumbs.

Cool on a wire rack. These keep for a day or two in an airtight container, or you can freeze them in foil for a couple of months. Just reheat from frozen at 150°C/130°C fan/gas mark 2 for 15 minutes for fresh muffins.

Wienerbrød – Danish pastry

When most people think of Scandinavian baking, they think of Danish pastries, although wienerbrød *(literally 'Viennese bread') actually originated in the Austrian city of Vienna. Over the years the Danish recipe was adapted to make it more flaky and crispy than other types of* vienoisserie *like croissants. The secret to successful Danish pastry lies in incorporating the butter in layers which puff up during baking, giving the distinctive flaky finish. The four classic Danish pastry recipes which follow all use the same base Danish dough (adapted from masterbaker Dan Lepard's recipe), which is then shaped and filled differently. I use 500g strong white flour which makes the dough easier to work but can be a little chewy – if you want a softer dough, use 50:50 plain flour and strong flour. Making Danish pastry requires a reasonable amount of time as it needs several periods of chilling, so you will need to prepare the dough the day before you want to bake the pastries.*

250-300ml whole milk
500g strong white flour
10g fine sea salt
2 tbsp caster sugar
2 tsp freshly ground cardamom
15g fresh yeast or 7g fast action dried yeast
1 medium egg, beaten
250g unsalted butter, chilled

Scald 250ml of the milk by heating it in a small pan until almost boiling and then allow it to cool. Scalding the milk makes the finished pastry softer.

Sift the flour, salt, sugar and cardamom together in a large bowl, sprinkle in the dried yeast (if using) and stir through. If using fresh yeast, cream it with a teaspoon of the sugar in a small bowl and once it is liquid (after about 30 seconds) add to the dry ingredients.

Make a well in the middle, add the beaten egg and then the milk mixture, which should be warm rather than hot to the touch, as otherwise you risk killing the yeast. Stir everything together until the mixture comes off the sides of the bowl, adding as much of the remaining milk as you feel is needed until the dough looks – for want of a better word – doughy. Shape in to a rough rectangle shape, cover with lightly oiled clingfilm and refrigerate overnight.

Take the dough out of the fridge and allow to come to room temperature (30-60 minutes depending on how cold your fridge is). Use a cheese slicer or a very sharp knife to cut 250g chilled butter in to thin slices, and place them on a rectangular sheet of baking parchment about 10cm x 25cm.

Lightly flour the surface you're going to roll the dough on and the dough itself. Roll out to a rectangle about 45cm x 15cm and roughly 1cm thick. Starting at one end of the pastry rectangle, put the parchment paper butter-side down on the pastry, leaving a border of a couple of centimetres around the edges. Gently peel back the parchment, leaving the butter in place so that two-thirds of the pastry is covered with it. Scrape off any butter left sticking to the parchment and smooth on to the buttered pastry, making sure the butter is evenly distributed and that there are no large lumps sticking out.

Fold the unbuttered pastry third over to sit on top of the half of the buttered pastry, and then fold the remaining buttered third on the top of that, so you end up with a rectangle of pastry a third of the size but three times as thick as when you started. Turn the pastry 90° and roll out again to a rectangle about 1cm thick. Fold in thirds lengthways again, cover with clingfilm and refrigerate for one hour.

Remove from the fridge, place on a lightly floured surface and roll in to a long rectangle (roughly 50cm x 10-15cm) when it again should be about 1cm thick. This time fold both the shorter ends in so they meet in the middle and then fold one half on top of the other, as if you're closing a book. Turn the pastry 90° and roll out again in to a rectangle about 1cm thick. Fold in thirds lengthways one last time, cover with clingfilm and leave to chill for another hour or so before using to make one of the following tasty Danish pastries.

Spandauer – custard-filled Danish pastries

This is the Danish pastry I remember most vividly from growing up in Norway, where it is called wienerbrød. *This is of course the generic name for all Danish pastries in Denmark, so both the baker and I were a little confused when I first tried to buy one when visiting Copenhagen! These custard-filled almond-topped pastries make a fabulous indulgent treat. They are traditionally finished with a drizzle of sugar icing – I find them sweet enough without it, but if you have a sweet tooth, feel free to drizzle away.*

MAKES 12-15

1 batch Danish pastry (page 114)
1 batch *skoleboller* custard (page 96) or 500ml ready-made fresh custard
1 medium egg, beaten
handful flaked or roughly crushed almonds

Lightly oil a large baking sheet or line with parchment paper. Roll out the chilled Danish pastry on a lightly floured surface until it forms a rectangle about 30cm x 40-50cm. Slice in to 12-15 equal-sized squares of pastry, about 10cm x 10cm each, and place about 3-4cm apart on the baking sheet.

Put a heaped spoonful of custard in the middle of each square of pastry. Gently fold the corners of each square in towards the middle, pressing gently so that they stay put, and brush the exposed pastry surfaces with beaten egg. Scatter almonds over the top, cover and leave to prove in a warm place for 20 minutes. While they are proving, preheat the oven to 220°C/200°C fan/gas mark 7.

Bake on the upper shelf for 5 minutes before reducing the heat to 190°C/170°C fan/gas mark 5 for a further 3-5 minutes or until they look golden brown and feel crispy and firm to the touch. Leave to cool slightly on a wire rack before eating, to avoid burning your mouth on the hot custard filling…

Frøsnapper – sesame and poppy Danish twists

These little poppy and sesame seed twists are a much-loved favourite with Danes and I defy anyone visiting Scandinavia to not fall in love with this twisty treat. It is filled with almond remonce, which is a sugary almondy buttercream. See the photo for how the finished twists should look.

MAKES 15

1 batch Danish pastry
  (recipe on page 114)
100g ground almonds
  (or whole almonds, blanched
  and ground)
100g caster sugar
50g butter, softened

3 tbsp flour or finely ground
  stale breadcrumbs
1 tsp vanilla extract
pinch of salt
1 medium egg, beaten for glazing
poppy seeds and sesame seeds
  for sprinkling

Roll out the chilled Danish pastry on a lightly floured surface until it is about 60cm x 40cm, then use a sharp knife to trim this in to a neat rectangle. Turn the pastry rectangle so that one of the 60cm-long sides is closest to you.

Mix the almonds, sugar, butter, flour or breadcrumbs, vanilla and salt together in a medium bowl to form the *remonce* paste. Spread the *remonce* over the half of the pastry closest to you, so that an area measuring roughly 60cm x 20cm is smoothly covered in the buttery filling. Fold the uncovered half of the pastry towards you so that it sits on top of the *remonce*-covered half, and press gently around the edges to seal in the filling. Glaze the surface with beaten egg and sprinkle on lots of poppy seeds, followed by plenty of sesame seeds (if you sprinkle the sesame seeds first, they tend to disappear under the poppy seeds!)

Lightly oil a large baking sheet, or line with parchment paper. Slice the pastry in to 15 strips, each about 4cm wide. Take the end of each strip and twist twice so the ends are seeded-side uppermost with an unseeded (underside) section showing in the middle of the two twists. Brush the unseeded sections with beaten egg. Place the twists about 3-4cm apart on the prepared baking sheet, cover and leave to prove in a warm place for 20 minutes. While they are proving, preheat the oven to 220°C/200°C fan/gas mark 7.

Bake on the upper shelf for 5 minutes before reducing the heat to 190°C/170°C fan/gas mark 5 for a further 3-5 minutes or until they look golden brown and feel crispy and firm to the touch.

Leave to cool on a wire rack for a little while (the *remonce* filling will be very hot) before enjoying – warm, buttery, flaky and utterly delicious.

VARIATION:

If you want a slightly flashier look, only use poppy seeds for the initial sprinkling then, after you've twisted the pastry and glazed the unseeded sections with beaten egg, sprinkle those parts with sesame seeds. This way you'll have twists that alternate poppy seeds and sesame seeds along their length for colour contrast.

Jam star Danish pastries

Little pinwheel jam stars look very pretty and are really easy to make. I like to use fruit of the forest jam but you can use any flavour – just make sure it's a thick chunky jam, not too runny or it will ooze out of the pastry during baking. These pastries are traditionally finished with a drizzle of sugar icing – I find them sweet enough without it, but feel free to embellish.

MAKES 12-15

1 batch Danish pastry (recipe on page 114)
12-15 tbsp jam
1 medium egg, beaten

Lightly oil a large baking sheet or line with parchment paper. Roll out the chilled Danish pastry on a lightly floured surface until it forms a rectangle about 30cm x 40-50cm. Slice in to 12-15 equal-sized squares of pastry, about 10cm x 10cm each, and place about 3-4cm apart on the baking sheet.

Use a sharp knife to split each corner of the squares by cutting a couple of centimetres in from the tip towards the centre, leaving the middle of each pastry square uncut (to make room for the jam).

Dollop a tablespoon of jam in the centre of each square. Lift one side (left or right, whichever you prefer) of one of the split corners of the pastry square and fold it in towards the middle, pressing gently in to the jam so that it stays put. Repeat with the same side of each of the remaining split corners, pressing the pastry tips together in the middle, to give a pinwheel star shape. Brush the exposed pastry surfaces with beaten egg (dabbing a little on the points where they meet in the middle to stick them together), cover and leave to prove in a warm place for 20 minutes. While they are proving, preheat the oven to 220°C/200°C fan/gas mark 7.

Bake on the upper shelf for 5 minutes before reducing the heat to 190°C/170°C fan/gas mark 5 for a further 3-5 minutes or until they look golden brown and feel crispy and firm to the touch. Leave to cool slightly on a wire rack and eat while still warm (but not immediately out of the oven, as the jam gets very hot).

Almond *kringle* wreath

Kringle, *a sweet enriched dough wreath or pretzel shape, gets its name from the Old Norse word for a ring or circle, and is a traditional treat found all across Scandinavia. My Norwegian grandmother used to make a variety of festive* kringler *filled with almond paste, custard or sticky jam. They're great for sharing at coffee-time or at an indulgent brunch, and are a real taste of old-school Scandinavian baking. It is traditional to shape the* kringle *in to a pretzel shape but it is easier to bake it as a wreath, as here – or just leave it as a long cylinder if you prefer. You can finish the* kringle *with icing if you want to make it look a little more traditional (try the icing for the lemon nutmeg madeleines on page 206 or a simple sugar glaze) but don't feel that you have to – it is perfectly delicious just as it is!*

MAKES 1 WREATH

Dough
300ml whole milk
75g butter
500g refined spelt (or plain) flour
100g caster sugar
1 tsp ground cardamom (optional)
¾ tsp fine sea salt
15g fresh yeast or 7g fast action dried yeast
1 medium egg, beaten

Filling
50g raisins
150g *mandelmasse* (50% almond paste) or marzipan
75g almonds, roughly ground
50g butter
1 tsp vanilla extract
1 medium egg, beaten
¼ tsp fine sea salt
caster sugar to taste

To finish
1 medium egg, beaten
flaked almonds
perlesukker sugar crystals, crushed sugar cubes or demerara sugar

Scald the milk by heating it in a small pan with the butter until it is almost boiling and then allow it to cool while you assemble the other ingredients. Scalding the milk makes the finished *kringle* softer.

Sift the flour, sugar, cardamom and salt together in to a large bowl, sprinkle the dried yeast in and stir through. If using fresh yeast, cream it with a teaspoon of sugar in a small bowl and once it is liquid (after about 30 seconds), add to the dry ingredients.

Make a well in the middle of the dry ingredients, add the beaten egg and then the milk-butter mixture, which should be warm rather than hot to the touch, as otherwise you risk killing the yeast. Stir everything together until the mixture comes off the sides of the bowl and looks – for want of a better word – doughy. Place the dough in a lightly oiled plastic bag or cover the bowl with lightly oiled clingfilm, and leave to rise in a warm place for 30 minutes.

Put the raisins in a small bowl, cover with water and leave to soak for 15 minutes before draining. While they are soaking, put all the other filling ingredients except the sugar in a medium-sized bowl and cream together (or blitz in a food processor). Then season to taste with caster sugar – I tend to add 2-3 tablespoons but feel free to use more if you have a sweet tooth.

Roll out the dough on a lightly floured surface until it forms a long, thin rectangle about 60cm x 15cm. Spread the filling evenly over it, starting from the middle and working outwards. If the buttery mix is a little cold, you can use your hands to spread it, as the heat helps to smooth the butter out (and it's immensely satisfying getting your hands all sticky). Drain the raisins and sprinkle evenly over the buttered dough. Then roll the dough in to a cylinder, rolling from one of the longer edges of the rectangle, brushing the other long edge with a little water to help seal the pastry. Bring the two open ends together to form a circular wreath shape and pinch to seal the open edges, so that the filling doesn't spill out.

Cover the *kringle* and leave to rise in a warm place for 20-30 minutes until it has doubled in size. You can test to see if it has proved enough by gently poking it with your little finger – the indentation should stay put.

Preheat the oven to 200°C/180°C fan/gas mark 6. Glaze the risen dough with beaten egg and sprinkle the flaked almonds and sugar over the top. Bake on the middle shelf of the oven for 30-40 minutes until golden brown and hollow-sounding when tapped on the base.

Cool on a wire rack before serving on the day of baking. Alternatively store in the freezer (for emergencies!) – then simply wrap in foil and defrost in a 150°C/130°C fan/gas mark 2 oven for about 20-25 minutes, before removing the foil and baking for a further 5 minutes at 190°C/170°C fan/gas mark 5, for crisp, warm, freshly baked *kringle* any time of day or night…

VARIATIONS

Try filling this with cinnamon butter (cinnamon bun-cake recipe, page 100) or cardamom butter (substitute ground cardamom for the cinnamon) instead of the almond filling. This is also delicious filled with a thick fruity jam such as raspberry or fruit of the forest. Just make sure that the jam isn't too runny, so you don't end up with soggy dough. Alternatively, spread about 250ml vanilla custard over the dough before rolling for a traditional filling. If you fancy making your own, try the *skoleboller* custard on page 96 – you'll need half a batch for the *kringle*.

You could also try making this as a saffron *kringle* by putting a few strands (about 0.5g) of saffron in the milk when it is heated with the butter, then leave to infuse for 10-15 minutes before making the dough.

Tebirkes – poppy seed Danish pastries

Tebirkes *are delicious poppy seed covered Danish pastries, a little like* pain au chocolat *in appearance, but with buttery almond* remonce *inside instead of chocolate. These are perfect for a lazy breakfast or brunch, but to be honest, they are delicious at any time of day…*

MAKES 12-15

1 batch Danish pastry (recipe on page 114)
100g ground almonds (or whole
  almonds, blanched and ground)
100g caster sugar
50g soft butter

3 tbsp flour or finely ground stale
  breadcrumbs
1 tsp vanilla extract
pinch of salt
1 medium egg, beaten for glazing
poppy seeds for sprinkling

Roll out the chilled Danish pastry on a lightly floured surface until it is about 30cm x 40cm, then use a sharp knife to trim this in to a neat rectangle.

Mix the almonds, sugar, butter, flour or breadcrumbs, vanilla and salt together in a medium bowl to form the *remonce* paste. Spread the *remonce* over most of the pastry, leaving a 2cm border around the edges. Carefully roll the pastry up, starting from the longest edge, until it resembles a long swiss roll, and position it so that the pastry 'seam' is on the bottom. Brush the top surface with beaten egg and sprinkle generously with poppy seeds.

Lightly oil a large baking sheet, or line with parchment paper. Use a sharp knife to cut the pastry in to 12-15 even slices, place about 3-4cm apart on the baking sheet, cover and leave to prove in a warm place for 20 minutes. While they are proving, preheat the oven to 220°C/200°C fan/gas mark 7.

Bake on the upper shelf for 5 minutes before reducing the heat to 190°C/170°C fan/gas mark 5 for a further 3-5 minutes or until they look golden brown and feel crispy and firm to the touch. Leave to cool on a wire rack for a little while (the *remonce* filling will be very hot) before enjoying with a good hot cup of coffee or tea.

Cakes

The restorative powers of good cake

never cease to amaze me: if you're feeling a bit down in the dumps, a slice of moist carrot cake or sticky ginger spice cake can really brighten your day. The Swedes have long recognised this, and even have their own word (*fika*) to describe a get-together with family or friends for coffee and a sweet treat, when you can sit and solve the problems of the world, or your corner of it at least.

Adding fruit is an excellent first step to creating great cake. Bake it in – as in blueberry upside-down cake or banana spice cake, or generously layer it in and on – like Norwegian strawberry, elderflower and vanilla *bløtkake*, and Danish raspberry, blueberry and passionfruit-lime *lagkage*, both constructed of tiers of light sponge and fabulous fillings to make them real winners for celebrations and parties.

When we're not adding fruit, Scandinavians are nuts about baking with nuts: almonds, hazelnuts, walnuts, coconuts… Tosca cake, with its light vanilla sponge and caramelised almond topping is the quintessential Scandi cake; flourless hazelnut and whisky chocolate cake is perfect for anyone who can't eat wheat; coconut igloo cake is a wonderfully wintry alternative to Christmas fruitcake; and pastel green marzipan-covered *princesstårta* is a brilliant celebration cake, whether you're royal or not.

Last but definitely not least, given my status as a confirmed chocoholic, there's a healthy(ish) helping of chocolate. From gooey traybake for children's birthdays to the decidedly more grown-up chocolate stout cake with whisky icing, there's something for all the family.

Toscakaka — caramel almond-topped sponge
Scandilicious bløtkake — strawberry,
  elderflower and vanilla cream cake
Lagkage — Danish layercake with raspberries,
  blueberries and passionfruit-lime curd
Princesstårta — Swedish princess cake
Upside-down blueberry and elderflower cake
Spelt banana bread
Banana spice cake
Scandilicious carrot cake
Sticky ginger spice cake
Birthday cake
Chocolate stout cake with whisky frosting
Chocolate and orange marmalade loaf cake
Flourless hazelnut and whisky chocolate cake
Coconut igloo cake

Toscakaka – caramel almond-topped sponge

Some believe that this cake is named after Puccini's Tosca, others that it is a reference to the almond cakes found in Toscana (Tuscany). Whatever the origins of the name, this is one of Scandinavia's most beloved cakes. It is a little flatter than the typical sponge cake but the buttermilk helps to keep it light and fluffy under the rich caramel-almond topping. If you can't get hold of buttermilk, just add half a teaspoon of lemon juice or white wine/cider vinegar to 75ml whole milk to sour it. I make the praline like a salted caramel, as I find the salt really brings out the nutty flavour.

SERVES 8-10

Sponge

3 medium eggs
150g caster sugar
½ tsp vanilla extract
150g plain flour
1 tsp baking powder
¼ tsp fine sea salt
75g butter, melted
75ml buttermilk

Praline

125g butter
125g light brown
 muscovado sugar
150g flaked almonds
50ml whole milk
¾-1 tsp fine sea salt
½ tsp vanilla extract

Preheat the oven to 170°C/150°C fan/gas mark 3-4 and lightly oil a 23cm round cake tin.

Whisk the eggs, sugar and vanilla extract in a large bowl (or mixer) until pale and fluffy. Mix the flour, baking powder and salt in a small bowl. Gradually add the melted butter, buttermilk and dry ingredients to the beaten egg mixture in stages, alternating between them and folding through with a large metal spoon as you go until everything is incorporated.

Gently pour the cake batter in to the prepared tin and tap it once or twice against the kitchen surface to pop any big bubbles which would make substantial pockets of air in the finished cake. Bake on the middle shelf of the oven for 25-30 minutes or until golden and firm to the touch.

Start preparing the topping about halfway through the baking time so that it is ready to use by the time the cake is cooked. Put all the topping ingredients in a medium saucepan over a low-medium heat and bring to a simmer, stirring all the while. Allow to simmer for 3-4 minutes to thicken slightly.

Remove the cake from the oven and turn the oven temperature up to 220°C/200°C fan/gas mark 7. Use the hot praline to glaze the sponge cake while still in its tin, then put the cake back on the upper shelf of the oven and cook a further 5-10 minutes until the topping is crispy and golden brown.

Allow to cool slightly in the tin before running a knife around the edges to separate the praline from the sides. Gently remove the cake from the tin and allow to cool on a wire rack before serving. This keeps well in an airtight container for 3-4 days.

VARIATIONS

If you're a coffee fan, the praline topping is delicious with a double shot of espresso in it.
Use coconut instead of flaked almonds to make this in to Danish *drømmekage* dream cake.

Scandilicious bløtkake – strawberry, elderflower and vanilla cream cake

This is my version of the traditional tiered celebration cakes made for birthdays and special occasions in Norway and Denmark. This cake is best eaten on the day you make it as the strawberries tend to become rather soft after that – alternatively you could use firmer berries like blueberries instead. The undecorated sponge freezes well, so can be made in advance and frozen until needed – simply defrost for a couple of hours at room temperature before using. I recommend making the custard yourself (skoleboller recipe, page 96) in advance of baking, but you can use ready-made fresh custard if you are short of time. You only need half a batch of skoleboller custard, so halve the quantities (or make the full amount and eat the leftovers later, as I do!)

SERVES 8-10

Sponge
4 medium eggs
150g caster sugar
½ tsp vanilla extract
150g plain flour
1 tsp baking powder
¼ tsp fine sea salt

Filling and topping
1 punnet fresh strawberries
elderflower cordial
½ batch *skoleboller* custard (page 96) or 250ml ready-made fresh custard
200g crème fraîche
2 tbsp icing sugar (optional)
fresh elderflowers or other edible flowers to garnish (optional)

Preheat the oven to 170°C/150°C fan/gas mark 3-4 and lightly oil a 23cm round cake tin with sides at least 5cm deep.

Put the eggs, sugar and vanilla in a large heatproof bowl set over a pan of simmering water and whisk until pale and fluffy. The mixture should look mousse-like and when you remove the whisk, the trail of mixture it leaves on the surface should remain visible for about 4 seconds. Sieve the flour, baking powder and salt in to a separate bowl. Add the flour mixture a third at a time to the beaten eggs, gently folding through with a large metal spoon each time to distribute evenly while taking care not to knock out all the air.

Carefully pour the cake batter in to the prepared tin and tap the tin once or twice against the kitchen surface to pop any big bubbles which would make substantial pockets of air in the finished cake. Bake on the middle shelf of the oven for 25-30 minutes or until golden and firm to the touch. Insert a skewer if you're unsure – it should come out clean with only a few crumbs on it and no uncooked cake mixture. Allow to cool for 5-10 minutes in the tin, then remove from the tin and leave to cool completely on a wire rack.

Hull and quarter most of the strawberries, leaving five nice-looking ones whole to garnish. Pour the elderflower cordial over the quartered strawberries in a small bowl and leave to macerate for 15 minutes or so before draining. Reserve the strawberry-elderflower cordial.

Insert a toothpick in to the side of the cake about halfway down and repeat on the opposite side, leaving at least half of each toothpick sticking out. Then use a cheese wire or a very sharp knife to slice the cake in half horizontally, using the toothpicks as your guide to see the halfway line. Carefully place the bottom half of the cake cut-side up on the plate or board on which you will be serving the cake, and put the top half cut-side down on a separate plate.

Shortly before you want to serve the cake (ideally no more than an hour in advance or it will go soggy), spread a smooth even layer of the vanilla custard over the cut surface of the bottom half of the cake. Carefully put a layer of drained strawberries on top and drizzle with a little of the elderflower cordial for extra flavour, if you wish. Sandwich the upper half of the cake on top (cut side downwards) and gently press down.

If you wish to sweeten the crème fraîche, whip it gently with the icing sugar – alternatively leave it unsweetened to give a tangy contrast to the other sweet layers. Spread the crème fraîche over the top of the cake and garnish with the reserved whole strawberries and artistically scattered flowers (if using).

Lagkage – Danish layercake with raspberries, blueberries and passionfruit-lime curd

This decadent three-layered sponge is my take on the classic Danish lagkage *or layercake, and is perfect for dinner parties or birthdays. The Danes traditionally use strawberries, cream or custard, marzipan and crushed macaroons to fill their* lagkage; *however, I love the sharp tang of exotic passionfruit-lime curd and the freshness of the mixed berries which together balance the delicate vanilla cream and sweet sponge. The passionfruit curd works beautifully with tropical fruit too – sliced kiwis, mango, passionfruit, guava, dragonfruit... whatever takes your fancy. There are no hard and fast rules about how you compile your* lagkage, *so feel free to mix up the layers with different combinations of curd, cream and berries – just make sure you leave enough cream and berries for the top. If you can't get hold of buttermilk, just add a teaspoon of lemon juice or white wine/cider vinegar to 100ml whole milk to sour it.*

SERVES 8

Sponge
4 medium eggs
250g golden caster sugar
1 tsp vanilla extract
150g butter, melted
100ml buttermilk
250g refined spelt
  (or plain) flour
1 tsp baking powder
¼ tsp fine sea salt

Passionfruit-lime curd
6 ripe passionfruit
juice of 3 limes
zest of 1 lime
75g caster sugar, plus
  more to taste
2 medium eggs
2 medium yolks
150g unsalted butter,
chilled and cubed

Topping
300ml whipping cream
1 tsp vanilla extract
3 tbsp caster sugar
1 punnet raspberries
1 punnet blueberries

Preheat the oven to 170°C/150°C fan/gas mark 3-4. Lightly oil three 20cm round cake tins and line each base with a circle of parchment paper.

Whisk the eggs, sugar and vanilla in a large bowl (or mixer) until pale and fluffy. When you remove the whisk, the trail of mixture it leaves on the surface should remain visible for 2-3 seconds.

Pour in half the melted butter and buttermilk, sift in half the flour and then use a large metal spoon to fold through from the bottom of the bowl to the top in swift figure-of-eight movements. The idea is to incorporate the liquids and flour as quickly as possible without knocking out all the air. Add the rest of the butter and buttermilk and sift in the remaining flour along with the baking powder and salt, then fold through again using the same figure-of-eight motion until the cake batter looks evenly mixed (don't worry if there are still a few small blobs of flour on the surface).

Pour a third of the batter in to each cake tin and tap the tins once or twice against the kitchen surface to pop any big bubbles which would make substantial pockets of air in the finished cake.

Bake on the middle shelf of the oven for 15-20 minutes or until the cakes have doubled in size, and are golden and firm to the touch. Insert a skewer if you're unsure – it should come out clean with only a few crumbs on it and no uncooked cake mixture. Allow to cool for 5-10 minutes in their tins, then remove from the tins and leave to cool completely on a wire rack.

Put all the ingredients for the passionfruit-lime curd apart from the butter in a heatproof bowl over a saucepan of simmering water and stir continuously with a whisk or wooden spoon until the mixture starts to thicken slightly. Add the cubes of butter one at a time, continuing to stir as they melt, until you have a glossy, thickened curd. If the mixture gets too hot it will start to look greasy. Keep some iced water nearby so that if this happens, you can stir in a few drops to stop the curd from splitting (if in doubt, take it off the heat altogether).

Once all the butter has been incorporated, taste the curd and stir in some more sugar to taste – I like to keep it relatively tart as a nice contrast to the sweetened cream and sponge. Remove from the heat and allow to cool completely.

Assemble the *lagkage* shortly before you want to serve it (ideally no more than an hour in advance). Whip the cream with the vanilla and sugar until very soft peaks form – you don't want to overwhip it, so just a quick whizz with an electric whisk or 30-60 seconds by hand should do it. Place one of the sponge layers on the plate or board on which you will be serving it (if it is domed from baking, you may want to turn it upside down). Tip about a third of the curd on the sponge base and spread in an even layer. Scatter a quarter of the berries over the curd and carefully place the second sponge layer on top. Spread this sponge with up to half the remaining curd followed by half the vanilla cream, sprinkle with a further quarter of the berries, then gently cover with the final layer of sponge. Finish by spreading the top with the remaining vanilla cream and generously covering with the rest of the berries.

This is one of my favourite ways to stack this cake, but you can layer the fillings however the fancy takes you! Serve as soon as possible after assembling.

The leftover curd can be stored for up to a couple of weeks in a sterilised jam jar – to sterilise, just wash the jar then dry it for 10 minutes in a 100°C/80°C fan/gas mark ¼ oven. This curd makes an excellent topping for toast, crumpets, pancakes, yoghurt …

Princesstårta – Swedish princess cake

This cake is thought to have been created for three Swedish princesses at the beginning of the 20th century. No one seems to know why the marzipan has to be delicate pastel green, but believe me, it does. Princesstårta is traditionally a layercake, but my simplified version is quicker and easier to make, while tasting just as good. The layer of tart jam balances the rich sweetness of the sponge, custard, cream and marzipan, while the popping candy adds a delightful crunch to what is otherwise a very soft cake, so do try this modern twist on a classic! I recommend making the custard yourself (half a batch of skoleboller custard, page 96) in advance of baking, but you can use ready-made fresh custard if you are short of time. If you can't get hold of buttermilk for the lagkage, just add half a teaspoon of lemon juice or white wine/cider vinegar to 50ml whole milk to sour it. This delightfully whimsical

but rather fragile confection requires a little patience and a lot of chilling (you and the ingredients) but it is beautiful, indulgent and definitely worth the effort!

SERVES 10-12

½ batch *lagkage* sponge mixture (page 135)
100g white chocolate, buttons or roughly chopped
40g popping candy
150g raspberry, blackcurrant or blackberry jam
½ batch *skoleboller* custard (page 96)
 or 250ml ready-made fresh custard, chilled
300ml double or whipping cream, chilled
2 tbsp caster sugar
400g marzipan
few drops green food colouring
pink marzipan rose or edible flowers to garnish
length of ribbon, about 2cm wide (optional)
icing sugar, to dust surface (optional)

Preheat the oven to 170°C/150°C fan/gas mark 3-4 and lightly oil a 23cm round cake tin and line its base with a circle of parchment paper.

Prepare half a batch of *lagkage* sponge batter and bake in the prepared tin, following the recipe up to and including cooling on a wire rack. An hour or so before you wish to serve, place the cooled sponge on a cake stand or serving plate, so that you can turn it with ease while decorating.

Melt the white chocolate in a heatproof bowl over a saucepan of simmering water – be careful not to stir too much or the chocolate may seize. Remove from the heat, then stir in the popping candy. Spread evenly over the surface of the sponge.

Tip the jam on to the middle of the cake and spread over the chocolate-coated surface, leaving about a centimetre around the edge uncovered, to prevent the darker-coloured fruit jam bleeding in to the green marzipan. If the jam is very liquid, you might want to pop the cake in the freezer for 30-45 minutes to set the jam before putting the custard on top.

Spoon the chilled custard in to a piping bag with a 1cm nozzle (or a freezer plastic bag with one corner sliced off to pipe through). Tilt the bag at a 45° angle to the top surface of the cake and pipe a smooth line of custard all the way around the edge of cake to form a ring on the jam-free rim. Pipe the rest of the custard over the middle of the cake on top of the jam and spread carefully to create an even layer.

Whip the chilled cream with the sugar to stiff peaks – it needs to hold its shape when the marzipan is placed on top – and spread over the custard using a palette knife or similar unserrated knife. Turn the cake stand or serving plate in a clockwise direction and gently use the knife to create as round a dome as you can. It's tempting to spend ages doing this but be decisive and the dome will take shape before you know it! Pop the cake in the freezer for 20-30 minutes to firm up the cream. It needs to be very cold and stiff, otherwise the marzipan will fall off or sink in and ruin the dome effect.

Roughly break up the marzipan, drizzle with a few drops of green food colouring and knead with your hands until it is a uniform pale pastel green. Different brands of food colouring vary in strength so do err on the side of caution as you don't want lurid neon green marzipan! Place the green marzipan on a clean work surface dusted with sieved icing sugar or between two sheets of baking parchment. Roll in to a circle about 3-4mm thick – don't make it too thin, otherwise it may tear when you place it on the cake.

Place the marzipan over the rolling pin, lift above the centre of the cake, then very gently drape over to cover it. Quickly but gently press the marzipan all over the cake for a uniform shape and trim off any excess, leaving about 1cm extra around the base to tuck carefully underneath the sponge to secure it.

Garnish with edible flowers – a pink marzipan rose is traditional but use what you like. If you're feeling extra girly, tie some pretty ribbon around the base, using a little blu-tack to hold the ends together. The cake will hold its shape for an hour or two at most before it starts to collapse, so serve as soon as possible with some fresh fruit and a cup of good tea or coffee.

Upside-down blueberry and elderflower cake

There is something gloriously nostalgic and retro about fruity upside-down cakes. I adore this blueberry one with its beautiful deep indigo colour, hint of elderflower and light sponge made with Greek yoghurt. This is a real crowd-pleaser, great for celebrations and special occasions. This cake doesn't keep well as the blueberries lose their fresh intensity relatively quickly after cooking, so be sure to get your friends around to enjoy it on the day of baking!

SERVES 8-10

400g fresh or frozen blueberries
50ml elderflower cordial
4 medium eggs
250g caster sugar
1 tsp vanilla extract
125g refined spelt (or plain) flour

125g ground almonds
2 tsp baking powder
¼ tsp fine sea salt
125g butter, melted
125g Greek yoghurt

Preheat the oven to 170°C/150°C fan/gas mark 3-4, and lightly oil a 23cm round cake tin (springform, if you have one). Wrap the outside of the tin in a layer of aluminium foil to create a tight seal, in order to prevent any blueberry juice leaking out. Spread the blueberries evenly over the base of the cake tin, drizzle with elderflower cordial and set aside to macerate.

Whisk the eggs, sugar and vanilla in a medium bowl (or mixer) for 5-8 minutes until pale and fluffy. When you remove the whisk, the trail of mixture it leaves on the surface should remain visible for 2-3 seconds. Combine the flour, almonds, baking powder and salt in a small bowl. Gradually mix the melted butter, yoghurt and dry ingredients in to the beaten egg mixture in stages, alternating between them, until you have a smooth, thick cake batter.

Pour the batter over the blueberries and bake on the middle shelf of the oven for 30-35 minutes or until the top looks golden and feels springy and firm to the touch. The sides should be slighty lifting away from the edges of the cake tin. Remove from the oven and allow to cool for 15 minutes in the tin before releasing the springform (if applicable), carefully flipping the cake upside down on to a plate so that the blueberries are facing upwards and removing the tin.

This cake is wonderful just as it is, or you could try it with a scoop of good vanilla or clotted cream ice cream, or perhaps a dollop of Greek yoghurt or crème fraîche.

VARIATIONS

Try this with raspberries, blackberries, mulberries, mixed summer berries, cherries, cloudberries or thinly sliced or quartered plums, apricots or rhubarb.
Apples work really well too, but be sure to cut in thin slices and fan them out on the bottom of the cake tin as this helps to cook them properly (plus it looks pretty!)

Spelt banana bread

This recipe came about when I was wondering what to do with some very ripe bananas and didn't fancy a traditional banana bread. So I rummaged through my cupboards and used what I could find. The result? A simple healthy(ish) banana bread that makes a great teatime snack or scrumptious breakfast treat. If you don't have any buttermilk, just use 100ml whole milk with a teaspoon of lemon juice or white wine/cider vinegar in it to sour it.

MAKES ONE LOAF

3 ripe medium bananas, mashed
100ml buttermilk
75g butter, melted
75ml maple syrup
1 medium egg
225g refined spelt (or plain) flour
50g wholemeal spelt (or wheat) flour
4 tbsp porridge oats, plus 1 tbsp for sprinkling
1½ tsp baking powder
¼ tsp bicarbonate of soda
½ tsp ground nutmeg
¼ tsp salt
100g chopped walnuts or pecans

Preheat the oven to 170°C/150°C fan/gas mark 3-4 and lightly oil a 900g loaf tin.

Stir the bananas, buttermilk, melted butter, maple syrup and egg together in a large bowl. Add all the other ingredients and fold in with a large metal spoon until evenly mixed. Pour the cake batter in to the loaf tin, smooth the top with a spatula and sprinkle with the additional tablespoon of oats.

Bake on the upper-middle shelf of the oven for 50-60 minutes until the loaf has doubled in size and looks golden brown. If in doubt, insert a skewer in the centre of the loaf – if there's any wet mixture on it when you take it out, bake for a few minutes longer. Allow to cool in the tin for 15-20 minutes then remove from the tin and leave to cool completely on a wire rack.

Banana bread keeps really well for 3-4 days in an airtight container or wrapped in clingfilm or aluminium foil. Perfect for breakfast, brunch, elevenses, afternoon tea, midnight feast snackage…

Banana spice cake

Banana cake is a relatively recent addition to the Scandinavian cake repertoire but, much like carrot cake, has been welcomed with open arms and looks set to stay. This is a simple, delicious cake which keeps really well for 3-4 days (the flavour actually improves after baking, so it's perfect for making ahead of time), as well as being a brilliant way to use up over-ripe bananas. What more could one ask?

SERVES 8-10

3 medium eggs
125g caster sugar
I tsp vanilla extract
3 very ripe medium bananas
juice of ½ lemon
100g light brown muscovado sugar
250g refined spelt (or plain) flour
2 tsp baking powder
½ tsp bicarbonate of soda
I tsp cinnamon
½ tsp ground cardamom
½ tsp ground nutmeg
¼ tsp ground cloves
½ tsp fine sea salt
125g butter, melted
100g crème fraîche
handful chopped walnuts (optional)

Preheat the oven to 170°C/150°C fan/gas mark 3-4. Lightly oil a 23cm round cake tin and dust with flour.

Whisk the eggs with the caster sugar and vanilla in a medium bowl (or mixer) for 8-10 minutes until pale and fluffy. Mash the bananas in a small bowl with the lemon juice. Mix the muscovado sugar, flour, raising agents, spices and salt in a separate bowl. Gradually fold the bananas, melted butter, crème fraîche, walnuts (if using) and dry ingredients in to the beaten egg mixture in stages, alternating between them. Stir through a few times until you have a nice, smooth cake batter.

Pour the batter in to the tin and bake on the middle shelf of the oven for about 35-45 minutes until the top is golden brown and the sides are slighty lifting away from the edges of the tin. A skewer inserted in the middle should come out completely clean of uncooked mixture.

Allow to cool in the tin for 15 minutes or so, then remove from the tin and leave to cool completely on a wire rack. This banana cake keeps really well for 3-4 days in an airtight container or wrapped in clingfilm or aluminium foil.

Scandilicious carrot cake

After years of experimenting and tweaking my recipe, I think this is everything a good carrot cake should be – light and moist with a hint of warming spices and not too sweet. The secret to a good consistency is to make an emulsion with the eggs and vegetable oil, which then creates a more stable mixture so that the carrots don't all sink to the bottom! I was taken by the idea of the zesty lemon topping suggested by my friend Mungo, so you can choose whether to make a traditional vanilla frosting or a lemon version – alternatively use a simple lemon icing (150g icing sugar mixed with the zest and juice of half a lemon) to glaze instead. It is then up to you whether you leave the cake as it is, or whether you decorate the top with little marzipan carrots, seasonal berries, unsweetened desiccated coconut or sliced kiwi (as my mother does).

MAKES 12 SLICES

4 medium eggs
125g caster sugar
125g light brown
  muscovado sugar
200ml vegetable oil
250g refined spelt
  (or plain) flour
2 tsp cinnamon
¼ nutmeg, freshly grated
2 tsp baking powder
½ tsp bicarbonate of soda
½ tsp fine sea salt
350g carrots, peeled
  and coarsely grated

Frosting

125g butter, softened
150g icing sugar
150g full fat cream cheese
2 tsp vanilla extract
  (or juice and zest
  of 1 lemon)

Preheat the oven to 170°C/150°C fan/gas mark 3-4 and lightly oil a 20cm x 30cm rectangular cake tin.

Whisk the eggs and sugars for a few seconds in a large bowl (or in a mixer) to break up the eggs, then continue to whisk (at medium-high speed if using a mixer) while slowly drizzling in the vegetable oil. It is worth being patient with this – if you add the oil in one go, the mixture will split.

Fold in the flour along with all the other ingredients apart from the carrots and stir through a few times. Add the carrots and gently stir a few times so that they are just incorporated, and pour the batter in to the prepared tin. Bake on the middle shelf of the oven for 40-45 minutes or until the cake looks golden brown and feels firm to the touch. Allow to cool in the tin for 15 minutes or so, then tip out on to a wire rack and leave to cool completely.

Cream the butter and icing sugar together in a bowl until pale. Add the cream cheese, vanilla (or lemon juice and zest) and a tiny pinch of salt and beat until smooth.

You can either ice the cake straight away or put the frosting in the fridge for an hour or so to firm up slightly before spreading evenly over the top and sides of the cake. This cake keeps well for 3-4 days in an airtight container in a dry, cool place (so the icing stays firm) – but not in the fridge, otherwise it will dry out.

Sticky ginger spice cake

As you will undoubtedly have noticed by now, we love our spices in Scandinavia. This luscious sticky spice cake keeps well for a week or two and is brilliant to have on standby in case you get unexpected guests popping round on the weekend or at teatime – and you might want to have a slice or two with a lovely hot cup of tea or spiced chai while you're waiting to see who turns up… If you can't get hold of buttermilk, just add 1½-2 teaspoons of lemon juice or white wine/cider vinegar to 250ml whole milk to sour it.

MAKES 12 SLICES

125g butter
175g molasses sugar (or dark brown muscovado)
150ml treacle
250ml buttermilk
2 medium eggs, lightly beaten
175g refined spelt (or plain) flour
75g wholemeal spelt (or wheat) flour
2 tsp bicarbonate of soda
1 tsp baking powder
2 tsp cinnamon
2 tsp freshly grated root ginger
1 tsp ground cardamom
½ nutmeg, freshly grated
½ tsp fine sea salt

Preheat the oven to 170°C/150°C fan/gas mark 3-4 and lightly oil a 900g loaf tin.

Melt the butter, sugar and treacle together in a medium saucepan, stir through, then remove from the heat and allow to cool slightly. Beat in the buttermilk and eggs. Mix the flours, raising agents, spices and salt in a medium bowl and gradually add to the liquid ingredients in the pan in stages, stirring thoroughly after each addition until evenly mixed.

Pour the dark thick cake batter in to the tin and bake on the middle shelf of the oven for 45 minutes, then cover the loaf with aluminium foil (to stop the top from burning) and bake for a further 15 minutes.

Allow to cool in the tin for 15 minutes or so, then remove from the tin and leave to cool completely on a wire rack. This cake tastes great on the day it's made but actually improves with age (the best things always do!) and will keep for up to two weeks tightly wrapped in clingfilm.

VARIATION

Try this cake glazed with a simple lemon icing (150g icing sugar mixed with the zest and juice of half a lemon) for a delicious flavour contrast.

Birthday cake

When we lived in Oslo, my friends' mothers would always seem to bake traybakes for their birthday cakes. As kids we loved eating the little chunky squares of cake topped with butter icing and sweets, and never noticed that we were almost certainly consuming a smaller amount than if we'd had a slice or two of a traditional round cake! Clever women, those Norwegian mothers…

MAKES 12 MEDIUM OR 16 SMALL SQUARES

5 medium eggs
250g light brown
  muscovado sugar
75g dark chocolate
150g butter, melted
50g cocoa powder
double shot of espresso
  or 60ml strong coffee
100g crème fraîche
3 tbsp milk
200g self-raising flour
¼ tsp fine sea salt

Icing

150g butter, softened
3-4 tbsp cocoa powder
150g icing sugar, sifted,
  plus more to taste
1 tsp vanilla extract
1-3 tbsp milk

Topping

(to be chosen by the
birthday boy or girl!)
Sweets or chocolates
  or unsweetened
  desiccated coconut

Preheat the oven to 170°C/150°C fan/gas mark 3-4. Lightly oil a 20cm x 30cm rectangular baking tin, or line it with two sheets of baking parchment laid at right angles to each other (this makes it easier to lift out the cake when baked).

Whisk the eggs and sugar in a large bowl (or mixer) for about 8-10 minutes until pale and fluffy. Melt the chocolate and butter in a heatproof bowl over a saucepan of barely simmering water. Put the cocoa in a cup or mug and stir in the hot espresso to create a sticky paste. Stir the crème fraîche and milk together in a jug or small bowl.

Gradually add the chocolate-butter, mocha paste, milk mixture, flour and salt to the beaten egg mixture in two stages, half at a time, whisking continuously on a low setting until everything is incorporated in an even batter.

Pour in the tin and bake on the middle shelf of the oven for 25-30 minutes until firm to the touch, checking towards the end of the baking time to see whether a skewer inserted in the middle comes out cleanly with no uncooked cake batter on it. Allow to cool in the tin for 15 minutes or so, then remove from the tin and leave to cool completely on a wire rack before icing.

Cream the butter in a medium bowl, then gradually sift in the cocoa powder and icing sugar while continuing to cream, using a spatula to scrape down any mixture that starts to climb the sides. Stir in the vanilla and one tablespoon of milk and mix until the icing has a smooth consistency. Taste and add more icing sugar if you think it needs it. The icing should hold its shape but not feel stiff – too stiff and the icing will be hard to spread, too loose and it will slide off – if in doubt, test a small dollop on the cooled cake to see how it fares. If the icing is too stiff, stir in some or all of the rest of the milk, as necessary, to loosen it.

Use a palette knife or other non-serrated knife to spread the butter icing over the cake, making sure to cover the sides and corners completely to seal in the sponge. Sprinkle with the birthday boy or girl's chosen topping, and don't forget the candles…

VARIATION

Make a mocha buttercream by using a single shot of espresso in place of the milk.

Chocolate stout cake with whisky frosting

Scandinavians love their beer, but while you sometimes find it featuring in bread baking, you seldom see it in cakes. I love the combination of chocolate and beer and this cake is a happy marriage of both. As for the frosting, well, whisky and cream is another dream combo and the pale foamy topping mimics the froth on a good glass of stout… although the cake is also delicious unfrosted. I use duck eggs as they work really well in sponges but you can of course use hen's eggs instead. The Norwegian brunost *(brown cheese), however, is mandatory. OK it's not, but do try it, as it just adds that little bit of caramel-umami-thoroughly-Scandi oomph.*

SERVES 8-10

250ml Guinness or stout
250g butter
50g cocoa powder
75g dark chocolate
30g *brunost*, grated
1 shot of double
  espresso or
  30ml strong coffee
150ml soured cream
2 medium eggs
350g light brown
  muscovado sugar
1 tsp vanilla extract
275g refined spelt
  (or plain) flour
2 tsp baking powder
½ tsp bicarbonate of soda
¼ tsp fine sea salt

Frosting
125g butter, softened
150g icing sugar
150g full fat cream cheese
3-4 tbsp whisky

Preheat the oven to 170°C/150°C fan/gas mark 3-4 and lightly oil a 23cm round cake tin.

Warm the Guinness, butter, cocoa, chocolate and *brunost* in a medium saucepan over a low-medium heat until melted together and foamy. Remove from the heat, stir in the espresso and soured cream and set aside.

Beat the eggs, sugar and vanilla in a medium-large bowl (or mixer) until pale golden and fluffy. Mix the flour, raising agents and salt together in a small bowl. Gradually whisk the Guinness mixture and dry ingredients in to the beaten eggs in stages, alternating between wet and dry and whisking as you go until everything is mixed together in a dark, smooth cake batter.

Pour the batter in the tin and bake on the middle shelf of the oven for 35-45 minutes or until the top of the cake feels springy and firm to the touch and a skewer inserted in the middle comes out cleanly. Allow to cool in the tin for 15 minutes or so, then remove from the tin and leave to cool completely on a wire rack before icing.

Cream the butter and icing sugar together until fluffy, then add the cream cheese, three tablespoons of the whisky and a tiny pinch of salt and beat until smooth. Taste to see how strong the whisky flavour is and add more to taste – I like it quite robust so tend to use all four tablespoons.

You can either ice the cake straight away or put the frosting in the fridge for an hour or so to firm up slightly before spreading evenly over the top of the cake, so that it looks like a glass of stout from the side! This cake keeps well for a couple of days stored in an airtight container.

Chocolate and orange marmalade loaf cake

My love of loaf cakes stems from childhood birthdays when Mama Johansen would bake a chocolate cake in a loaf tin, cover it with chocolate buttercream and decorate it with Freia Non-Stop (Norway's answer to Smarties). Somehow chocolate cake always tasted better as a loaf! I use honey to sweeten the cake, but you can use 200ml golden syrup or 200g brown sugar instead. The marmalade gives a delicious hint of Jaffa cake, and I love to eat this squidgy moreish cake with a small glass of Grand Marnier, either drizzled over it or sipped alongside, for a grown-up treat.

MAKES 1 LOAF

200g refined spelt
  (or plain) flour
50g ground almonds
2 tsp baking powder
¼ tsp bicarbonate of soda
½ tsp fine sea salt
2 medium eggs,
  lightly beaten
200ml clear honey
  (or 250ml if you have
  a sweet tooth!)
2 tbsp plain yoghurt
1 tsp vanilla extract
50g cocoa powder
1 shot espresso
  or 2 tbsp strong coffee
200ml orange marmalade
juice (approx. 75ml)
  and zest of 1 large or
  2 small oranges
100g butter, melted
75g orange-flavoured
  dark chocolate, chopped,
  or chocolate chips
  (optional)

Preheat oven to 180°C/160°C fan/gas mark 4 and lightly oil a 900g loaf tin.

Mix the flour, ground almonds, raising agents and salt together in a large bowl. Mix the eggs, honey, yoghurt and vanilla together in a smaller bowl. Put the cocoa in a cup or mug and stir in 100ml boiling water and the coffee. Tip the marmalade in to another small bowl and mix with the zest and juice.

Make a well in the middle of the dry ingredients and pour in the melted butter, egg mixture, cocoa-coffee mixture and half the marmalade mixture (you'll need the rest to glaze the cake after baking). Stir until smooth – there should be no pockets of flour remaining – then stir in the chocolate (if using).

Pour the batter in the tin and bake on the middle shelf of the oven for 30-40 minutes until firm to the touch. Check to see whether the cake is cooked after 30-35 minutes by inserting a metal skewer in the centre: it should come out cleanly with no uncooked batter on it.

Allow to cool in the tin for 20 minutes, then turn out on a wire rack and leave to cool completely. Place the cooled cake on a serving plate or cake board and use a skewer to make lots of holes through the top down in to the cake, taking care not to go all the way through the base. Slowly pour half the remaining marmalade glaze over the surface of the loaf cake, making sure it trickles down the skewered holes in the cake before drizzling the top with the rest of the marmalade glaze.
This cake keeps well for 2-3 days in an airtight container.

Flourless hazelnut and whisky chocolate cake

Chocolate and whisky have a real affinity for each other and work together extremely well in this deliciously indulgent cake. I've used ground hazelnuts as I think they taste wonderful with the chocolate, but you can substitute ground almonds (or flour) if you prefer. I like to serve this with whisky-spiked whipped cream, or even some ice cream drizzled with whisky. Hic.

SERVES 8-10

4 medium eggs
250g caster sugar
100g butter, melted
50ml whisky
50g cocoa powder, plus more to finish (optional)
2 tsp baking powder
¼ tsp vanilla salt
200g ground hazelnuts
icing sugar to finish (optional)

Preheat the oven to 180°C/160°C fan/gas mark 4 and lightly oil a 23cm round cake tin.

Whisk the eggs and sugar in a large bowl (or mixer) for 5-8 minutes until pale and fluffy. Continue to whisk as you gradually add the melted butter, whisky and cocoa in stages, alternating between them until they are fully incorporated. Tip in the baking powder, vanilla salt and hazelnuts and stir to bring the mixture together, but don't overwork it otherwise the nuts will leach their oil.

Pour the batter in the tin and bake on the middle shelf of the oven for 35-40 minutes. Test that it is fully cooked by inserting a metal skewer or knife tip – there should be no uncooked mixture on it when you withdraw it.

The cake will collapse a little after you remove it from the oven, but don't worry, this is perfectly normal. Remove from the tin and allow to cool on a wire rack before dusting the top with cocoa or icing sugar (if using). This keeps well for 4-5 days in an airtight container or wrapped in foil or clingfilm.

Coconut igloo cake

This cake makes a great edible Christmas gift – it keeps well for 2-3 days, children love the igloo shape and it's a great alternative to the ubiquitous fruit cake! You can hire or buy specialist cake tins for making the igloo – my favourite is the non-stick version by NordicWare. You can bake the cake ahead of time, wrap it in aluminium foil and freeze until needed. To defrost, reheat in the foil at 150°C/130°C fan/gas mark 2 for 15-20 minutes, then simply remove the foil and leave to cool completely on a wire rack before applying the frosting and coconut. You need full fat cream cheese for the frosting, as lower-fat versions tend to split (and don't taste as nice!)

SERVES 8-10

150g unsalted butter, softened
200g caster sugar
150g light muscovado sugar
4 medium eggs
350g self-raising flour
½ tsp baking powder
1 tsp freshly grated nutmeg
1 tsp cinnamon
½ tsp fine sea salt
120ml whole milk
4 tbsp soured cream
4 tbsp strong coffee or double shot of espresso

Frosting

150g unsalted butter, softened
200g full fat cream cheese
150g icing sugar
1 tsp vanilla extract
50g unsweetened desiccated coconut (or white chocolate flakes)

Preheat oven to 180°C/160°C fan/gas mark 4. Lightly oil the igloo cake tin and dust with flour.

Cream the butter and sugars together in a large bowl until pale. Add the eggs one by one with a tablespoon of the flour each time to prevent the mixture splitting, whisking thoroughly after each addition. Mix the rest of the flour, the baking powder, the spices and the salt in a medium bowl. Mix the milk, soured cream and coffee together in a jug. Stir the dry and liquid ingredients in to the butter-egg mixture one-third at a time, alternating between wet and dry until everything has been incorporated in a thick cake batter.

Pour the batter in the cake tin – it should be about three-quarters full. Bake on the middle shelf of the oven for 40-50 minutes until a skewer inserted in the middle comes out clean of any cake mix. Allow to cool in the tin for 10 minutes or so, then carefully remove and leave to cool completely on a wire rack.

Mix the butter with the cream cheese, then stir in the icing sugar and vanilla and combine thoroughly. If the cake is completely cool, you can either ice it straight away or put the frosting in the fridge for an hour or so to firm up slightly before spreading evenly over the top and sides and sprinkling with coconut. Blissful with a steaming hot cup of coffee or strong builder's tea.

This cake keeps well for 2-3 days in an airtight container in a cool place (so the icing stays firm) – but not in the fridge, otherwise it will dry out.

Puddings and tarts

I tend to gravitate towards pudding baking

in the cooler months of the year, when autumnal days bring a crisp bite to the air and tempt you to don a Nordic jumper and curl up on the sofa to read the weekend papers or a good book while a baked pudding fills the house with its irresistible aroma. Fragrant cardamom and coconut rice pudding, soothing Swedish apple and almond pudding, creamy barley pudding with a hint of whisky… you'll find some real winter warmers.

But puddings aren't just for the winter months – you'll find fantastic puds for warm weather in here too, from traditional tarts like Norwegian spiced almond *fyrstekake* to flower-strewn boozy cherry and pistachio pavlova and my *Scandilicious* version of key lime pie.

Fruit tends to take centre stage in Scandi puddings – plump blueberries speckle oven-baked pancakes, juicy plums and blackberries make the perfect partner to crumbly spelt crisp topping, roasted rhubarb balances the richness of rice pudding, and ruby redcurrants add both flavour and a jewel-like beauty to traditional almond *mazarin* tart.

I love to give traditional recipes a little twist to make them my own or bring them up to date – try baked custards flavoured with zesty lemon verbena – but sometimes you just have to acknowledge that a classic dish is a classic for a reason. Take my childhood favourite, the deceptively simply but delicious *suksessterte* (success tart) which marries rich vanilla custard with a nutty macaroon base. It's one of the few recipes I haven't changed at all and for good reason – you don't mess with perfection!

Fruit of the forest basket

Swedish apple and almond pudding

Blackberry and plum spelt crisp

Pistachio pavlova with boozy cherries

Cardamom and coconut rice pudding
with roasted rhubarb

Baked barley pudding

Baked lemon verbena custards with rye granola

Finnish blueberry and buttermilk oven-baked pancake

Ostkaka – Swedish baked cheesecake

Suksessterte – Norwegian vanilla cream 'success tart'

Redcurrant mazarin tart

Fyrstekake – Norwegian spiced almond tart

Scandilicious key lime pie

Fruit of the forest basket

A lovely simple dessert which makes the most of seasonal summer berries baked in a pastry basket – wonderful with a dollop of crème fraîche or a scoop of really good vanilla ice cream. I make this with a mix of raspberries, blueberries, blackberries, cherries, redcurrants and/or blackcurrants, but do try it with plums, gooseberries, apples and pears too.

SERVES 6-8

110g unsalted butter, softened
110g caster sugar
250g plain flour
2 tsp baking powder
¼ tsp fine sea salt
75ml soured (or double) cream
1 medium egg, separated
450g mixed berries
juice and zest of 1 lemon
6 tbsp fructose (or 9 tbsp caster sugar)
caster sugar, to finish (optional)

Mix the butter and sugar in a large bowl until just combined. Add the flour, baking powder and salt and quickly mix until it resembles breadcrumbs (you can do this by hand or using a food processor). Add the soured cream and egg yolk and mix with your hands or in a processor until the pastry comes together. Remove from the bowl, place on a sheet of clingfilm and shape in to a disc about 20cm in diameter. Wrap in the clingfilm and chill in the freezer for 15 minutes or so.

While the pastry is chilling, wash the berries (if they need it) and tip them in to a large bowl. Add the lemon juice, zest and fructose and gently stir through to coat the berries.

Preheat the oven to 200°C/180°C fan/gas mark 6. Take the pastry out of the freezer, place between two sheets of baking parchment or silicone paper and roll out until it is about 5mm thick – you don't want the pastry to be too thin or it may split. If the pastry gets too soft while you are rolling it out, just pop it back in the freezer for 5 minutes, as soft pastry will be difficult to handle when filling with fruit.

Gently place it in a 23cm cake tin or pie form. You don't have to push it in to the corners, as a loose form looks best when baked. Tip the sweetened fruit in to the pastry and carefully fold over the edges, crimping them slightly as you go – the pastry edges should cover about a third of the fruit. Lightly beat the egg white and use to glaze the pastry, then sprinkle with sugar (if using) for a little extra crunch.

Bake in the oven for 25-30 minutes until the fruit is bubbling and the pastry is light golden brown and cooked through.

Serve from the tin while still warm.

Swedish apple and almond pudding

The original recipe and inspiration for this delicious cakey-pudding came from my Swedish friend Christina, and it was only after I had baked it a couple of times that I remembered that my mother used to make a very similar apple dessert when I was a child. I like to use Bramley cooking apples in this, as their tartness is in a lovely contrast to the buttery sponge, but feel free to use other crunchy apples instead. If you're feeling decadent, you could mix a splash of calvados in to the whipped cream to serve with this, or just enjoy a little glass alongside.

SERVES 6-8

2 apples
½ tsp cinnamon (optional)
juice of ½ lemon
2 medium eggs
125g caster sugar, plus more for sprinkling
½ tsp vanilla extract
30g plain flour
75g ground almonds
1 tsp baking powder
100g butter, melted
pinch of fine sea salt
50g flaked almonds

Preheat the oven to 200°C/180°C fan/gas mark 6 and lightly butter a 20cm pie dish.

Peel and core the apples, slice in to eighths and scatter inside the pie dish. Sprinkle on the cinnamon (if using) and the lemon juice to prevent the apples oxidising too much while you prepare the pudding batter.

Whisk the eggs, sugar and vanilla in a medium bowl for about 5 minutes or until pale and fluffy. Add the flour, ground almonds, baking powder, melted butter and salt, and mix together. Pour this mixture over the apples, smooth the top and sprinkle with the almond flakes. Finish with a generous dusting of caster sugar before baking on the upper-middle shelf of the oven for 25-30 minutes or until golden brown and firm to the touch.

Serve warm just as it is or with lightly whipped cream.

Blackberry and plum spelt crisp

Blackberries and plums are popular across Scandinavia. They tend to come in to season around the same time and they go together beautifully in this pudding. The tart fruit flavours are balanced by the sweet pomegranate molasses and the crispy crumble-like topping, to which I add spelt flakes for a slightly nutty taste. You can ring the changes by substituting different types of flour and flakes or adding nuts and seeds, but do keep the ratio of flour to butter the same, as a great crispy topping is all about proportions.

SERVES 6-8

Crisp
150g unsalted butter, chilled
200g refined spelt (or plain) flour
100g spelt or oat flakes
1 tsp vanilla extract
150g caster or demerara sugar
½ tsp fine sea salt

Filling
800g plums, de-stoned
400g blackberries
6 tbsp pomegranate molasses
4 tbsp fructose (or 6 tbsp caster sugar)
juice of 1 lemon
butter, chilled, to top (optional)

Roughly grate the butter and then either rub it in to the flour and flakes by hand or blitz with them in a food processor until the mixture resembles breadcrumbs. Add the vanilla, sugar and salt and stir together, or blitz again if you're using a mixer. Tip the mixture on to a small tray and put in your freezer to chill for 5-10 minutes while you prepare the filling.

Preheat the oven to 200°C/180°C fan/gas mark 6. Slice the plums in quarters (or eighths if they are very large), put them in a roasting tin (roughly 20cm x 30cm) with the blackberries and drizzle the pomegranate molasses on top, stirring as you go. Stir in the fructose and the lemon juice and mix thoroughly.

Take the topping out of the freezer and use your hands to scrunch up thimble-sized balls of mixture. Scatter these over the fruit, as these granola-esque little clusters really add to the crunch factor of the topping. Once the fruit is well covered, sprinkle on the last of the topping mixture and dot with a few nuggets of butter (if using).

Bake on the upper-middle shelf of the oven for 25-30 minutes, keeping an eye on the topping – if it starts to take on too much colour, reduce the temperature to 180°C/160°C fan/gas mark 4. When it's ready, the topping should look golden brown and the juices from the fruit should be bubbling and oozing up around the edges. Allow to cool for a few minutes (so that the filling doesn't burn the roof of your mouth!) then serve with crème fraîche, Greek yoghurt or ice cream.

Pistachio pavlova with boozy cherries

Although originally Australian rather than Scandinavian in origin, I just couldn't leave a fruit pavlova out of this book. I always think pavlova looks so festive and celebratory, particularly when heaped high with an abundance of fresh seasonal fruit. This is a pretty riotous pudding with mallowy vanilla and pistachio meringue, liqueur-soaked cherries, tangy pomegranate molasses, crème fraîche, lightly whipped cream and a scattering of bright colourful edible flowers – pansies, nasturtiums, cornflowers, borage, marigold, cowslip, lavender, sweet violet – but put them all together and you have a sensational dinner party dessert!

SERVES 6-8

Meringue
4 medium egg whites
225g caster sugar
1 tsp cornflour
1 tsp white wine vinegar
1 tsp vanilla extract
75g unsalted shelled
  pistachios, crushed

Filling and topping
450g whole fresh cherries
450ml cherry liqueur
  (or cherry cordial)
170ml double cream,
  chilled
200ml crème fraîche,
  chilled
2 tbsp caster sugar,
  plus more to taste
50ml pomegranate molasses
assorted edible flowers
  (optional)
handful unsalted shelled
  pistachios, crushed,
  to garnish

Preheat the oven to 180°C/160°C fan/gas mark 4 and line a baking sheet with baking parchment or silicone paper.

Whisk the egg whites in a clean large bowl until they form stiff peaks. Add the caster sugar a couple of spoonfuls at a time and whisk each time to stiff peaks before adding more. When all the sugar is incorporated, whisk in the cornflour, white wine vinegar and vanilla extract and then carefully fold in the crushed pistachios.

Scoop the meringue mixture on to the baking sheet and smooth in to a circle about 23-25cm in diameter. Use a spatula to swirl the mixture around, creating dips and flicks of meringue here and there, and hollow out a shallow dip in the middle, about 15cm across, for the filling to sit in once the meringue is baked.

Place the meringue in the oven and immediately turn down the heat to 120°C/100°C fan/gas mark ½. Bake for 1¼ to 1½ hours and then switch the oven off completely, leaving the meringue to dry out and cool in the oven for several hours or overnight. While the meringue is cooling, put the cherries in a small bowl, pour the cherry liqueur over them and leave to soak for a couple of hours.

When you're ready to assemble the pavlova, lightly whip the double cream and crème fraîche together with the sugar until the cream thickens and just starts to hold its shape. Taste and add more sugar if you think it needs it – but do remember the meringue will be sweet too. Use a large spoon to scoop the whipped cream gently in to the centre of the pavlova and smooth it out to create an even layer.

Drain the cherries, keeping the liqueur for cocktails or to lace ice cream. Perch the boozy cherries on top of the cream, scattering a few around the sides for artistic purposes. Drizzle with the pomegranate molasses, garnish with edible flowers (if using) and sprinkle with the crushed pistachios for a little nutty crunch. Serve immediately.

If you don't fancy pistachio meringue, simply leave them out and make a plain vanilla meringue or substitute other nuts, such as almonds or hazelnuts, instead.

Instead of cherries, try making this with spiced cooked plums, greengages, apricots, peaches, nectarines, summer berries or (for a more exotic twist) passionfruit, lime zest and coconut shavings.

Strawberries and Cornish clotted cream make a fabulous classic topping for vanilla pavlova. Or try chocolate whipped cream (just add cocoa and sugar to the cream) on a vanilla, chocolate or nut pavlova base – it's seriously good topped with summer fruit or bananas.

Cardamom and coconut
rice pudding with roasted rhubarb

Rice pudding is a popular Scandinavian winter warmer, although it is often made on the stove top, like rice porridge, rather than baked. It is traditionally topped with a pat of butter and a liberal sprinkling of sugar and cinnamon; however, it is equally good with plum, sour cherry or cloudberry jam. This fragrant creamy oven-baked version goes beautifully with the slightly tart roasted rhubarb. It isn't overly sweet, so I like to add a little maple syrup or demerera sugar along with the rhubarb when serving. Using coconut milk adds flavour and makes this pudding dairy-free, but you can of course use whole milk instead if you wish.

SERVES 4-6

2 tbsp coconut oil
5 cardamom pods
100g pudding rice
1 litre coconut milk
3 tbsp caster sugar
3 stalks rhubarb
3 tbsp fructose (or 4½ tbsp caster sugar)
demerara sugar to sprinkle (optional) and/or to serve
maple syrup to serve

Preheat the oven to 150°C/130°C fan/gas mark 2. Heat the coconut oil in a medium saucepan over a low-medium heat. Slightly crush the cardamom pods so that they are partly open, then stir them in to the oil. Tip in the rice and stir thoroughly to coat in cardamom-infused coconut oil. After 2-3 minutes' stirring add the coconut milk and caster sugar and turn up the heat, continuing to stir so the rice doesn't stick to the bottom. Bring the mixture to the boil and then pour it in to a 20cm x 30cm roasting tin or equivalent sized heatproof dish. You may wish to remove the cardamom pods at this stage.

Put the pudding on the middle shelf of the oven to bake for an initial 30 minutes. While the rice is baking, slice the rhubarb in 5cm-long chunks and put in a bowl with the fructose. Stir and leave to macerate until the pudding has had 30 minutes, then drain the rhubarb and place on a baking sheet, reserving the macerating juices.

Stir the rice pudding and return to the oven (you can sprinkle demerara sugar on top after stirring if you want a crispy surface, but it's not essential). Put the rhubarb in to roast alongside the pudding and bake them both for 30 minutes.

Drizzle the roasted rhubarb with the reserved macerating juices and serve alongside or on top of the creamy rice pudding. Finish with a drizzle of maple syrup or a sprinkle of crunchy demerara sugar and dig in!

Baked barley pudding

*This is perfect comfort food, with its creamy texture, warming spices and hints of buttery vanilla.
It uses one of my favourite grains – barley – although you can use other grains like spelt or oats or
substitute barley flakes for pearl barley if you prefer: just reduce the cooking time to 30 minutes before
stirring and 30 minutes thereafter. This pud is one to warm the cockles on cool autumn evenings or
after chilly winter days outdoors. Great with a snifter of whisky or a mug of steaming hot, rich cocoa.*

SERVES 6-8

100g pearl barley
1 litre whole milk
25g butter
3 tbsp whisky (optional)
3 tbsp light brown muscovado or demerara sugar,
  plus more for sprinkling
1 small cinnamon stick or 1 tsp ground cinnamon
½ nutmeg, freshly grated
1 strip of lemon peel
200ml crème fraîche
1 medium egg yolk
plum jam or maple syrup to serve (optional)
sultanas, dates, sour cherries or prunes to garnish (optional)
hazelnuts or almonds to garnish (optional)

Bring the barley to the boil in a medium saucepan with plenty of lightly salted water and
simmer for 15 minutes. Drain and then stir in the milk, butter, whisky (if using), sugar,
spices and lemon zest. Keep stirring while you cook over a medium heat for a further
15 minutes until the barley feels quite soft but not cooked all the way through. Preheat the
oven to 170°C/150°C fan/gas mark 3-4 while the barley is cooking. Then remove the pan
from the heat, take out the cinnamon stick and lemon zest (or leave them in, as I do!) and
fold in the crème fraîche and egg yolk.

Lightly butter a 20cm x 30cm rectangular heatproof dish or 6-8 medium ramekins if you
want to serve individual portions. Tip the barley mixture in to the dish or ramekins and
bake in the oven for one hour if baking a single pudding or 20-25 minutes if baking individual
puddings. Remove from the oven, stir and sprinkle the top(s) with a few spoonfuls of sugar
before baking for a further 30 minutes for a single pudding or 15 minutes for individual ones.

Serve warm just as it is, or top with plum jam or maple syrup and a sprinkling of dried
fruit and nuts (if using).

Baked lemon verbena custards with rye granola

Lemon verbena is a wonderfully aromatic twist on the usual vanilla custard, and the crispy rye granola on top adds a little Scandi crunch. It's worth making a full batch of granola as it keeps well for a week or so in an airtight container, and is delicious sprinkled on yoghurt or over muesli. This pudding is perfect to prepare in advance – then simply bake the custards while you and your friends or family enjoy the rest of the meal. I like to serve these with jam or compote alongside, but they're great with fresh blueberries, redcurrants and raspberries too.

SERVES 6-8

200g stale rye bread
75g brown or
  demerara sugar
50ml coconut oil
1 tsp cinnamon
pinch of vanilla salt
500ml crème fraîche
20g lemon verbena leaves
zest of ½ lemon
6 medium egg yolks
50g caster sugar,
  plus more to taste
jam
  (ideally cloudberry)
  or fruit compote
  to serve

Preheat the oven to 200°C/180°C fan/gas mark 6 and line a baking sheet with parchment paper.

Blitz the rye bread in a food processor or break up by hand until you have small crumbs. Combine the rye crumbs, brown sugar, coconut oil, cinnamon and vanilla salt in a large bowl and stir well. Spread the mixture out evenly on the baking sheet and bake for 15 minutes. Allow the granola to cool completely and crisp up.

Turn the oven down to 150°C/130°C fan/gas mark 2 and boil a kettle of water.

Bring the crème fraîche, lemon verbena and lemon zest to a simmer in a medium saucepan. As soon as the mixture comes to the boil, remove from the heat and leave to infuse for 10-15 minutes.

Put the egg yolks in a large bowl. Sieve some of the warm crème fraîche mixture over them, then add the caster sugar and whisk to temper the yolks – this helps to keep the mixture from splitting. Sieve the remainder of the crème fraîche in and whisk well to combine. Taste and add more sugar if you think it needs it. Pour the custard in to medium-sized ramekins (about 7.5cm diameter) or ceramic dishes and pop them in a large 5cm-deep baking tray or roasting tin. Place on the middle shelf of the oven and then carefully pour hot water in to the tray or tin until it reaches about 3cm up the sides of the ramekins. Bake for 30 minutes or so until the custards are set but still have a slight wobble.

Serve warm, topped with a good sprinkling of rye granola and a dollop of jam or compote.

VARIATIONS

Make this dessert with classic vanilla custard – just use 1 teaspoon of vanilla extract or half a scraped vanilla pod and seeds instead of the verbena leaves and lemon zest.
For a spicy twist, infuse the crème fraîche with a cinnamon stick, 3-4 cardamom pods, half a fresh nutmeg (grated) and/or 2-3 cloves instead of the verbena leaves and lemon zest.

Finnish blueberry and buttermilk oven-baked pancake

Finnish baked pancakes, pannukakku, *are a wonderful tradition and are usually served with jam or fresh fruit. Oven-baking pancakes sounds a little odd if you are used to French-style crêpes, but is immensely practical when you're cooking for more than two. Baking rather than frying also makes them healthier – well, until you pile them high with crème fraîche and maple syrup, as I do! If you can't get hold of buttermilk, just add 2 teaspoons of lemon juice or white wine/cider vinegar to 284ml whole milk to sour it.*

SERVES 4

150g refined spelt (or plain) flour
25g oat bran
3 tbsp caster or light brown sugar
1 tsp baking powder
pinch of bicarbonate of soda
½ tsp fine sea salt
284ml buttermilk
2 medium eggs

25g butter, melted
1 tsp vanilla extract
200g blueberries, frozen or fresh
maple syrup to serve
cinnamon to serve
crème fraîche (or soured cream
  or Greek yoghurt) to serve

Put the flour, oat bran, sugar, raising agents and salt in a medium bowl and stir to distribute. Pour the buttermilk in a measuring jug and make up to 500ml with cold water. Crack the eggs in to a jug or a bowl and break up with a fork, then add the buttermilk-water mixture, melted butter and vanilla extract and stir through. Make a well in the middle of the dry ingredients and slowly drizzle in the liquid mixture, whisking constantly to create a smooth batter. Leave to rest for 30 minutes.

Preheat the oven to 220°C/200°C fan/gas mark 7. Lightly oil a 20cm x 30cm rectangular cake tin, roasting tin or heatproof dish and dust with flour. Scatter the blueberries over the bottom of the tin, pour the batter on top and bake on the upper middle shelf of the oven for 25-30 minutes until golden and firm to the touch. Check after 20 minutes – if the pancake is taking on quite a bit of colour, move it to the middle shelf and reduce the temperature to 200°C/180°C fan/gas mark 6.

Allow to cool slightly before dividing in to squares. Serve with a drizzle of maple syrup, a sprinkle of cinnamon and a dollop of crème fraîche on top.

VARIATIONS

Use raspberries or a mix of summer berries instead of blueberries.
Leave out the berries altogether for a traditional *pannukakku,* and top with jam or compote and some whipped cream.
Try adding a spritz of lemon and a drizzle of pomegranate molasses for an extra-tangy topping.

Ostkaka – Swedish baked cheesecake

In Sweden and Finland you find some really scrumptious cheesecakes and curd tarts. Traditional ostkaka *seems to be a Scandinavian cousin of the Yorkshire curd tart and, like its cousin, often contains raisins. This citrussy version uses lemon instead of dried fruit, which adds a fresh twist to the creamy curd. Using ground almonds instead of flour means that this dessert is gluten free.*

SERVES 6-8

4 medium eggs, separated
100g caster sugar, plus 1 tsp for the egg whites
200g fromage frais (or quark)
200g crème fraîche
1 tsp vanilla extract
50g ground almonds
zest of 1 lemon
juice of 2 lemons
¼ tsp fine sea salt
fresh fruit or plum jam to serve

Preheat the oven to 160°C/140°C fan/gas mark 3 and butter or lightly oil a 23cm round cake tin or similar sized ceramic baking dish.

Beat the egg yolks with the sugar in a large bowl until pale and fluffy, then gradually fold in the fromage frais, crème fraîche, vanilla, almonds, lemon zest and juice until fully combined.

Beat the egg whites with the salt in a medium bowl until stiff peaks form, add the teaspoon of sugar and whisk again to stiff peaks. Add one large tablepoon of the whisked egg whites to the egg yolk mixture and fold through to loosen it, then gently fold in the rest of the whites, being careful not to knock out all the air.

Spoon the cheesecake mixture in to the prepared cake tin or dish and smooth the top with a spatula. Bake on the middle shelf of the oven for 30-40 minutes or until the surface feels firm and looks golden. Serve warm with some fresh fruit or plum jam.

Suksessterte – Norwegian vanilla cream 'success tart'

Also known less romantically as 'yellow cream tart', I don't know why this is called 'success tart' – although it certainly seems to be a success with everyone who eats it. I first tasted this irresistible vanilla tart at a family wedding years ago. It is essentially an almond and egg white base with a rich buttery egg custard topping – very yin and yang. This tart freezes well if you want to prepare it in advance or have any left over, but trust me: once you've tried the sweet taste of success (tart), it's very difficult not to eat the whole thing in one sitting!

SERVES 6-8

Base
5 medium egg whites
200g icing sugar
200g ground almonds
1 tsp baking powder
¼ tsp fine sea salt

Topping
150ml double cream
100g caster sugar
5 medium egg yolks
200g cold salted butter, cut in 1cm cubes
1 tsp vanilla extract
cocoa powder for dusting (optional)

Preheat the oven to 170°C/150°C fan/gas mark 3-4 and lightly oil a 23cm round cake tin.

Whisk the egg whites with a pinch of salt in a large bowl until stiff peaks form.
Add the icing sugar a few spoonfuls at a time and keep whisking until stiff peaks form again. Put the ground almonds in a separate bowl with the baking powder and salt and stir well. Gently fold the egg white in to the dry ingredients until just blended – you don't want to knock all the air out but you don't want big blobs of egg white either.

Pour gently in to the prepared cake tin, smooth with a spatula and bake on the middle shelf of the oven for 30-35 minutes or until the base looks golden and feels firm to the touch. It may sink slightly after you remove it from the oven but don't worry, that's normal. Leave to cool in the tin on a wire rack while you prepare the topping.

Bring the double cream to a simmer in a saucepan, stir in the caster sugar and allow to dissolve completely before removing from the heat. Put aside to cool slightly. Lightly beat the egg yolks in a medium, heatproof bowl. Stir a couple of spoonfuls of the warm sweetened cream in to the yolks to warm them through, then pour in the rest of the cream and stir vigorously to create a smooth, creamy custard.

Pour the custard in to a saucepan (either the rinsed cream pan or a fresh one) and stir over a low heat until it thickens enough to coat the back of the spoon. If in doubt, run your finger through the custard on the spoon – your finger should leave a clear line. As soon as it has thickened, remove the pan from the heat and place on a cool surface. Gradually incorporate the butter cubes, whisking vigorously as you fold them in. If the mixture cools too much, simply pour in to a heatproof bowl, place over a pan of simmering water and keep whisking as you add the butter cubes. Once the butter is fully incorporated, stir in the vanilla extract, then pour the filling in to a medium bowl and cover with clingfilm directly on the surface to stop a skin forming. Once it has cooled slightly, place the filling in the fridge and chill until it is thick and stiff (about an hour or so).

Remove from the fridge and beat the filling with a spatula to soften it slightly before spreading on the almond tart base. Smooth the top of the tart and put back in the fridge to chill for at least an hour. Serve lightly dusted with cocoa powder (if using).

You can freeze this tart if you are making it ahead of time – just take out of the freezer and defrost in the fridge overnight before you want to serve it.

VARIATIONS

Sprinkle cinnamon or chocolate flakes over the tart instead of cocoa powder.
Garnish with *Daim* balls – indulgent but completely delicious.
Top with toasted, chopped almonds instead of or in addition to cocoa.
Try adding a teaspoon of cinnamon, cardamom or nutmeg to the almond base mixture if you fancy a different flavour.

Redcurrant *mazarin* tart

This golden mazarin *tart, jewelled with ruby redcurrants, comes courtesy of Norwegian food writer Hanne Stensvold. Mazarin is a typically Danish filling for tarts and pastries, although you also find it in Sweden. It is essentially Scandinavian frangipane, made with high almond content marzipan instead of the usual ground almonds. It's a delicious filling for any fruit tart – the Danes often pair* mazarin *with strawberries and it's lovely with blackcurrants or raspberries too – but the combination of sweet almondy* mazarin *and tart redcurrants always seems to me to work best. If you are making this tart by hand (rather than using a food mixer), you may want to beat the eggs lightly before incorporating them in the pastry and filling mixtures.*

SERVES 6-8

Pastry

200g refined spelt
 (or plain) flour
100g butter
50g caster sugar
1 medium egg

Filling

340g almond paste
 or marzipan
 (minimum 50%
 almonds)
100g butter, softened
100g plain flour
 (or cornflour)
6 tbsp caster sugar
2 tsp vanilla extract
4 medium eggs
300g redcurrants,
 rinsed and de-stalked

Blitz the flour and butter together in a food processor, or mix by hand in a large bowl, until it resembles breadcrumbs. Blitz or mix in the sugar and then the egg, and continue to blend or mix until the pastry dough comes together. Put the pastry on a sheet of clingfilm and shape in to a disc about 1cm thick. Wrap in the clingfilm and put in the fridge for an hour, or the freezer for 20-30 minutes, to chill.

Preheat the oven to 190°C/170°C fan/gas mark 5. Roll the chilled pastry out on a lightly floured surface until it is about 2.5cm thick (or as thin as you can roll it before it starts to crack) and about 28cm in diameter. The thinner the pastry, the crisper it will bake. Lift the rolled pastry in to a 23cm pie dish, cake tin or tart case and gently press in to the sides and edges. Trim any excess pastry from the rim. Prick the base of the pastry case with a fork, line with parchment paper, weigh down with rice or baking beans and bake on the middle shelf for 20-25 minutes or until golden brown. Leave to cool completely before filling.

While the pastry is baking, put all the filling ingredients apart from the redcurrants in a blender, mixer or medium bowl. Blitz or mix together until the *mazarin* is smooth and even, and all the ingredients have been fully incorporated.

Turn the oven temperature up to 200°C/180°C fan/gas mark 6. Pour the *mazarin* filling in to the pastry case and sprinkle the redcurrants over the top, gently pushing some of them in to the *mazarin* mixture. Bake on the middle shelf for 20-25 minutes until golden and well risen. Allow to cool slightly before eating just as it is, or with a spoon or two of crème fraîche.

Fyrstekake – Norwegian spiced almond tart

Norwegian fyrstekake, or prince's cake, is an old family favourite, as we are nutty (forgive the pun) about almonds and marzipan. This festive tart is made with an old-fashioned pastry that includes baking powder and double cream for an extra light, crisp texture. The filling is almond-based with a hint of aromatic cardamom. You can of course leave out the cardamom to make a simple almond-vanilla filling, or you can flavour it with a different spice (try cinnamon or nutmeg) or with some fresh citrus zest.

SERVES 8-10

Pastry

110g unsalted butter, softened
110g caster sugar
250g plain flour
2 tsp baking powder
¼ tsp fine (or finely crushed) sea salt
75ml double cream
1 medium egg yolk

Filling

2 medium egg whites
50g butter, melted
200g icing sugar
200g ground almonds
1 tsp ground cardamom
1 tsp vanilla extract
¼ tsp fine (or finely crushed) sea salt

To finish

1 medium egg yolk, beaten, to glaze
icing sugar to dust (optional)

You can make this pastry in a mixer or food processor or by hand. Mix the butter and caster sugar until just combined (you don't need to cream them). Add the flour, baking powder and salt and combine until the mixture resembles breadcrumbs. Add the double cream and egg yolk and mix until the pastry comes together. Divide the pastry in two (roughly 75:25 split) and shape in to two discs, one about 15cm in diameter, the other about 5cm. Wrap in clingfilm and chill in the fridge for an hour (or in the freezer for 15 minutes or so) while you make the filling.

Preheat the oven to 170°C/150°C fan/gas mark 3-4. Whisk the egg whites in a large bowl until stiff peaks form. Mix the remaining filling ingredients in a separate bowl and then fold in a third of the whisked whites to loosen the mixture. Gently fold in the remainder of the whites to create a light mousse and set aside.

Remove the pastry discs from the freezer – if they feel very hard, allow them to sit at room temperature for 3-5 minutes until the pastry softens slightly. Roll out the two discs until each is roughly 3mm thick. Use your rolling pin to lift the larger disc in to a 23cm round cake tin or pie tin. Press the pastry gently in to the sides and edges, then trim any excess from the rim.

Spoon the filling in to the pastry case. Cut the smaller pastry disc in to 2cm wide strips and place these across the top of the filling in a criss-cross lattice pattern. Glaze the lattice with beaten egg before baking the tart on the middle shelf of the oven for 50 minutes to an hour.

Allow the tart to cool completely in the tin then gently dust the latticework with icing sugar (if using). I like to eat this with a dollop of crème fraîche and some fruit compote or sliced clementines.

Scandilicious key lime pie

I first tried traditional key lime pie in Maine during the sort of summer when the bottoms of your flip-flops seem to melt on contact with the scorching tarmac. It is – whisper it – a no-bake pie, perfect for sultry days when you can't face cooking over a hot stove. Simply mix, chill and serve. Hallelujah. This 'scandified' version uses Swedish pepperkaker *(thin spiced biscuits) for the base – you can either make your own (see page 189) or use shop-bought ones for speed and convenience. Serve this with a refreshing pitcher of minty iced tea or, even better, a mint julep.*

SERVES 6-8

200g *pepperkaker*
125g butter, melted
30g unsweetened desiccated coconut
½ tsp cinnamon
7 limes
200g crème fraîche
370ml condensed milk, plus more to taste

Place the biscuits in a large plastic bag and crush with a rolling pin or large spoon until they resemble breadcrumbs – if you have a food processor you can of course blitz them, but bashing them is strangely satisfying. Put in a large bowl and add the melted butter, coconut and cinnamon. Mix thoroughly, then tip in to a 23cm pie tin or cake tin (or 6-8 medium ramekins, if you wish to make individual pies) and press down firmly until you have an even base layer. Pop in the freezer to chill it quickly.

Zest and juice six of the limes. Put the crème fraîche in a medium-large bowl, add the zest and stir for a minute before stirring in the condensed milk and juice. As soon as you add the lime juice the mixture will thicken, as the acidity of lime juice coils up the proteins in the condensed milk and crème fraîche. Taste the filling – it should be tangy but at the same time sweet enough that the lime juice isn't puckering your cheeks and making you wince. Add some of the juice of the remaining lime if the mixture is too sweet, or more condensed milk if it's too sour. Pour the filling on to a chilled pie base, smooth with a spatula, cover with clingfilm and refrigerate for a few hours or, better still, overnight to set.

When you're ready to serve the pie, run a round-ended knife or palette knife around the edge to release it – you can then remove from the tin (if using a springform) or serve it in the tin. Garnish with the zest of the remaining lime or sprigs of fresh mint. Any left-over pie will keep in the fridge for a few days – although you may find, as I do, that there is never any left over…

Biscuits, treats and edible gifts

Scandinavian Christmas – *jul,*

as in yuletide – involves plenty of traditional baked goods and delicious spiced and buttery biscuits. My Norwegian grandmother always made an early start on her Christmas baking, mixing, rolling and cutting out seemingly endless Norwegian festive biscuits from late November onwards, which kept us in baked goodies well in to Lent.

Pepperkaker spice biscuits are perhaps the best known of all our Christmas biscuits (thanks largely to the Swedish ones sold in IKEA) and their flavour improves over time, making them perfect to give as a present. Other delights include iced clementine butter biscuits and Swedish rye shortbread to hang on the tree, melt-in-the-mouth Norwegian vanilla-almond *serinakaker* and sticky Finnish spiced prune *joulutorttu* tarts.

If you fancy something a little different, try my caramel *brunostkjeks*, made with Norwegian brown cheese, or chewy marzipan *kransekake*, which traditionally graces weddings and new year celebrations across Scandinavia, but tastes so good that it deserves to be made far more regularly. Plus there's something for chocolate fans big and small – chocolate rice puffs are perfect for children's parties or teatime treats, while Danish *romkugler* rum truffles make a brilliant edible gift with a distinctly grown-up flavour.

Alongside these classic recipes, you will find other contemporary biscuits and edible gifts – how about home-made hazelnut brownies to accompany your cuppa; salted caramel *flappenjacken* bars stuffed full of oats, coconut and almonds for a twist on the traditional flapjack; or buttery madeleines flavoured with lemon and nutmeg or whisky? Whatever the time of year, whichever treats you choose to bake, I hope you'll find them thoroughly *Scandilicious*!

Clementine butter biscuits
Pepperkaker – Scandinavian spiced Christmas biscuits
Ginger and lemon biscuits
Chocolate cardamom biscuits
Serinakaker – Norwegian vanilla and almond butter biscuits
Rågkakor – Swedish rye shortbread biscuits
Flappenjacken – salted caramel granola biscuits
Toasted oat, date and hazelnut cookies
Brunostkjeks – Norwegian brown cheese biscuits
Joulutorttu – Finnish Christmas jam stars
Scandilicious kransekake – baked marzipan macaroons
Whisky madeleines
Lemon nutmeg madeleines
Chocolate hazelnut brownies
Norwegian chocolate rice puffs
Romkugler – Danish rum truffles

Clementine butter biscuits

I used to love making butter biscuits with my grandparents in Bergen when we visited at Christmas. The key to success with these is to keep the dough well chilled – the colder the dough, the crisper and lighter the biscuits. Royal icing is traditionally made with raw egg whites; however, since these biscuits are likely to be scoffed by small children, I use packet royal icing mix containing pasteurised whites. You can add a few drops of food colouring to the icing if you wish, but I like the contrast of the simple white icing against the green pine needles. In addition to the ingredients below, you will need some ribbon or silver / gold string to hang these on the Christmas tree.

MAKES ABOUT 20

350g plain flour
¾ tsp fine (or finely crushed) sea salt
250g unsalted butter, well chilled
125g icing sugar
zest of 2 clementines
1 medium egg yolk, lightly beaten
1 tsp vanilla extract
1 tsp milk or water (if needed)
300g packet of royal icing
30g edible silver balls

Mix the flour and salt in a large bowl, grate in the butter and combine using your hands until the mixture resembles breadcrumbs. Stir in the icing sugar and clementine zest and then add the egg yolk and vanilla extract and bring it all together. If the dough feels dry, mix in the teaspoon of milk or water to soften it. Divide the dough in two, shape in rounds, wrap in clingfilm and place in the freezer to chill for 30 minutes.

Remove the dough from the freezer and leave to come to room temperature for 10 minutes. In the meantime, preheat the oven to 170°C/150°C fan/gas mark 3-4 and line two baking trays with parchment paper.

Roll the dough out with a floured rolling pin on a lightly floured surface until roughly 3mm thick, then use a pastry cutter to cut out star, heart or other festive shapes. Each biscuit will need a small hole to thread ribbon or string through later, so use a sharp pointed knife to cut out a little circle (about 3-5mm across) near the top edge of each one. Place on the baking trays and bake for 10-15 minutes until golden. Allow the biscuits to cool completely on a wire rack before icing.

Make up the royal icing in accordance with the instructions on the packet and then ice the biscuits using a piping bag or small spoon. You can cover the biscuits with a simple smooth blanket of icing or you can get arty with lines, wiggles, criss-crosses, dots… let your imagination run riot! Dot the icing with silver balls and allow to set completely before tying loops of ribbon or string through the holes and hanging your festive biscuits on the tree.

Pepperkaker – Scandinavian spiced Christmas biscuits

Pepperkaker, or 'pepper cakes', get their name from the warming black pepper that was traditionally mixed in with the other spices. Many modern recipes leave it out, but I've included a smidgeon for old times' sake. You can cut these in stars, hearts, moons, Christmas trees – whatever takes your fancy – personally I have a soft spot for the classic round shape and traditional hearts. Do chill the dough overnight as it really helps with rolling it out thinly, plus it gives the flavours time to develop. This dough freezes well, so you can bake half now and freeze the rest to bake another day.

MAKES 35-40

150g unsalted
  butter, softened
150g caster sugar
70ml treacle
50ml golden syrup
75ml whole milk
1 medium egg yolk
450g plain flour
2 tsp ground ginger
2 tsp cinnamon
1 tsp ground
  cardamom
1 tsp bicarbonate
  of soda
½-1 tsp ground cloves
¼ tsp finely ground
  black pepper
½ tsp fine sea salt

You can use a food processor to make this dough or mix it by hand. Cream the butter and sugar together until pale and fluffy. Mix the treacle, golden syrup, milk and egg yolk together in a bowl or jug, and stir 400g flour and all the other dry ingredients together in a separate bowl. Alternate between adding wet and dry ingredients in stages, mixing as you go, until the dough comes together. Add some or all of the remaining 50g flour if the mixture seems too wet, although you want it to be quite sticky – it will set when refrigerated.

Divide the mixture in two and wrap in clingfilm, squishing and smoothing the mixture down as you seal it up until you have a round disc about 10cm wide. Refrigerate overnight or freeze until needed.

Allow the dough to come to room temperature for about 15-20 minutes. If you are using frozen dough, you will need to let it defrost overnight in the fridge beforehand.

Preheat the oven to 170°C/150°C fan/gas mark 3-4 and line two or three large baking sheets with baking parchment. Roll out the biscuit dough with a floured rolling pin on a lightly floured surface until it is roughly 2mm thick. The thinner you roll it, the crisper the biscuits will be – but if the dough gets too thin, the biscuits may be tricky to transfer to a baking sheet. You may find it easier to roll the dough directly on to the baking sheet and cut out the biscuit shapes there, lifting off the excess dough to roll out for the next batch.

Bake on the middle shelf of the oven for 8-10 minutes or until golden brown and crisp. Allow to cool on a wire rack while you repeat the rolling, cutting and baking until all the dough is used up. If you find that the cooled biscuits are still a little soft, you can always pop them back in a 150°C/130°C fan/gas mark 2 oven to dry out.

Properly crisp and dried out, these biscuits can keep in an airtight container for several weeks. My grandmother used to keep them from Christmas all the way through until Lent, but mine are always eaten up long before that! If the stored biscuits start to go soft, reheat them on a wire rack at 150°C/130°C fan/gas mark 2 for 5-10 minutes, then allow to cool completely on the wire rack once out of the oven to crisp them back up.

Ginger and lemon biscuits

These biscuits are a twist on the traditional spiced Scandinavian Christmas biscuits, and were inspired by my love of honey, ginger and lemon tea – sweet, soothing, spicy and warming. They make a lovely gift and are easily made gluten-free by using rice flour or gluten-free flour.

MAKES 20-30

125g salted butter, soft
125g caster sugar
1 medium egg
50ml golden syrup
50g crystallised ginger, chopped
1 tbsp freshly grated root ginger
zest and juice of 1 lemon
200g plain flour
1 tsp baking powder
¼ tsp bicarbonate of soda

You can use a food processor to make this dough or mix it by hand. Cream the butter and sugar together in a bowl until pale and fluffy. Mix the egg, golden syrup, crystallised ginger, grated ginger, lemon zest and juice together in another bowl or jug, and stir the flour and raising agents together in a third bowl. Alternate between adding wet and dry ingredients in stages, mixing as you go, until the dough comes together. Place in a smaller, clean bowl, cover with clingfilm and refrigerate for 1½-2 hours.

Preheat the oven to 190°C/170°C fan/gas mark 5 and line two baking sheets with baking parchment.

Use a teaspoon to place little dollops of biscuit mixture on a baking sheet, taking care to space them about 4-5cm apart, so they don't all merge during baking. Bake on the upper middle shelf for 8-10 minutes and allow to cool on a wire rack.

These keep well in an airtight container for up to a couple of weeks. If the stored biscuits start to go soft, reheat them on a wire rack at 150°C/130°C fan/gas mark 2 for 5-10 minutes, then allow to cool completely on the wire rack once out of the oven to crisp them back up.

VARIATION

Add 50g chopped pistachios in to the biscuit dough before chilling for a nutty version.

Chocolate cardamom biscuits

These biscuits are inspired by London chocolatier Rococo's heavenly dark chocolate speckled with cardamom. The combination of fragrant cardamom and seductive chocolate is just perfect to my mind, but these biscuits are also delicious without the spice. Alternatively, if you fancy a deeper darker flavour, you could add a shot of espresso coffee along with the vanilla extract. However you make them – spiced, mocha-ed or plain chocolate – a bag of these biscuits makes a brilliant gift for a chocoholic...
I often divide the dough in two before wrapping in clingfilm and chilling, so that I can put half straight in the freezer to bake another day – just defrost in the fridge overnight before you want to use it.

MAKES ABOUT 30

200g plain flour
50g cocoa powder
1 tsp ground cardamom
1 tsp baking powder
¼ tsp bicarbonate of soda
½ tsp fine sea salt
150g unsalted butter, chilled
150g light brown muscovado sugar
1 medium egg
1 tsp vanilla extract

You can use a food processor to make this dough or mix it by hand. Combine the flour, cocoa, cardamom, raising agents and salt in a large bowl or food processor. Grate in the chilled butter and mix or pulse until the mixture resembles breadcrumbs.

Stir or blitz in the sugar, then add the egg and vanilla, mixing again until the dough comes together. Put the dough on a long sheet of clingfilm, lightly fold one side of the sheet over it and roll in the clingfilm until it forms a long sausage shape roughly 3cm in diameter. Wrap tightly in the clingfilm, twisting the ends to get it really tight and to create a uniform sausage shape, and chill in the fridge for an hour or two (or in the freezer for 20-30 minutes) until the dough feels firm to the touch.

Preheat the oven to 190°C/170°C fan/gas mark 5 and line two baking trays with baking parchment. Unwrap the dough and use a sharp knife to slice carefully in to about 30 evenly sized discs, placing them a couple of centimetres apart on the baking trays as you go. If you don't want to bake all 30, just cut as many as you need and freeze the remaining mixture in clingfilm for another day.

Bake on the upper-middle shelf of the oven for 8-10 minutes – the biscuits should have risen slightly. Don't be tempted to bake them for too long or they will lose their potent cocoa flavour. Cool on a wire rack. You can keep these in an airtight container for up to a couple of weeks. If the stored biscuits start to go soft, reheat them on a wire rack at 150°C/130°C fan/ gas mark 2 for 5-10 minutes, then allow to cool completely on the wire rack once out of the oven to crisp them back up.

Serinakaker – Norwegian vanilla and almond butter biscuits

Serinakaker are one of the seven traditional biscuits typically baked at Christmas in Norway. Personally I don't think we should restrict our enjoyment of these delicious butter biscuits to yuletide as they taste fantastic all year round, so feel free to bake whenever! Delicious on their own or sandwiched in pairs with a spoonful of almondy remonce (page 116) for a decadent treat. I often divide the dough in two before wrapping in clingfilm and chilling, so that I can put half straight in the freezer to bake another day – just defrost in the fridge overnight before you want to use it.

MAKES ABOUT 30

200g plain flour
2 tsp baking powder
¼ tsp sea salt,
  finely crushed
150g butter, cold
  and cubed
125g caster sugar
1 medium egg,
  lightly beaten
1 tsp vanilla extract
1 tsp milk or water
  (if needed)
1 medium egg white,
  lightly beaten
sugar crystals or
  demerara sugar
  to sprinkle
finely chopped
  almonds (with skin
  on) to sprinkle

You can use a food processor to make this dough or mix it by hand. Combine the flour, baking powder, salt and butter in a mixer or a large bowl until the mixture resembles breadcrumbs. Stir or blitz in the caster sugar, then add the egg and the vanilla extract and combine until the mixture starts to come together. Mix in a teaspoon of milk or water if the dough feels dry and crumbly – it should feel soft but not sticky.

Place the dough on a long sheet of clingfilm. Lightly fold one side of the sheet over the dough and roll in the clingfilm until it forms a long sausage shape roughly 3cm in diameter. Wrap the dough-sausage tightly in the clingfilm, twisting the ends to get it really tight and to create a uniform sausage shape, and chill in the fridge for an hour or two (or in the freezer for 20-30 minutes) until the dough feels firm to the touch.

Preheat the oven to 200°C/180°C fan/gas mark 6 and line two baking trays with baking parchment. Take the dough out of the fridge (or freezer) and unwrap. Use a very sharp knife to slice in to about 30 evenly sized discs, placing them a couple of centimetres apart on the baking trays as you go. Glaze the tops with egg white and scatter with a generous sprinkling of sugar and chopped almonds.

Bake on the upper middle shelf of the oven for 8-10 minutes or until the biscuits have risen slightly, look golden and feel light when picked up. Allow to cool on a wire rack.

These biscuits should last a couple of weeks in an airtight container, but they're so moreish that you'll be lucky to see them stretch a week! If the stored biscuits start to go soft, reheat them on a wire rack at 150°C/130°C fan/gas mark 2 for 5-10 minutes, then allow to cool completely on the wire rack once out of the oven to crisp them back up.

Rågkakor – Swedish rye shortbread biscuits

These buttery rye biscuits come courtesy of my Swedish friend Tine who runs the Cambridge Cookery School. The recipe was handed down from her great aunt Thyra, who was a legend within the family for her amazing biscuits and other Swedish specialities. You can make these to hang on the Christmas tree, give to friends as gifts or just enjoy with a cuppa.

MAKES ABOUT 24

140g plain flour
40g rye flour
100g unsalted butter, chilled and cubed
60g caster sugar

Preheat the oven to 180°C/160°C fan/gas mark 4 and line a couple of baking sheets with parchment.

You can use a food processor to make this dough or mix it by hand. Combine the flours and the butter until the mixture resembles breadcrumbs. Add the sugar and then bring together, lightly working the dough until it is smooth.

Roll out the dough on a lightly floured surface until it is roughly 2mm thick, then use a round biscuit cutter to cut out discs, placing them on the baking sheets as you go. Gather up the excess dough, form in a ball and repeat the rolling and cutting process to use it all up. If the dough gets too warm, pop it in the fridge to chill again before baking, as otherwise your biscuits may be tough.

Use a fork to pierce each disc gently several times – and if you intend to hang these on the Christmas tree, cut a small hole (about 6-7mm wide) just in from the edge, through which you can later thread ribbon or string. Bake for 8-10 minutes until slightly golden, then cool on a wire rack.

These will keep in an airtight container for up to a couple of weeks. If the stored biscuits start to go soft, reheat them on a wire rack at 150°C/130°C fan/gas mark 2 for 5-10 minutes, then allow to cool completely on the wire rack once out of the oven to crisp them back up.

Flappenjacken – salted caramel granola biscuits

I can't claim that these are authentically Scandinavian in any way, but they are inspired by my love for salted caramel, Norwegian crispy havreflarn *oat biscuits and British flapjacks, or* flappenjacken *as the Muppet Show's Swedish Chef likes to call them! I don't know about his recipe but this one really hits the spot. The vanilla salt is essential, otherwise you'll end up with rather bland cereal biscuits, so if you don't have any, just use good flaked sea salt and a splash of vanilla. I like to use a mixture of equal parts oats, spelt, rye and barley flakes, but feel free to change the grains or the proportions to taste.*

MAKES ABOUT 20

150g unsalted butter
200g light brown muscovado sugar
100ml whole milk
1 medium egg
175g refined spelt (or plain) flour
175g mixed oats, spelt, rye and barley flakes
50g slivered almonds
25g unsweetened desiccated coconut
3 tbsp golden syrup
2 tsp vanilla sea salt
1 tsp baking powder

Heat the butter, sugar and milk in a medium-large saucepan over a medium heat until the butter has melted and the sugar has dissolved. Remove from the heat and stir in all the other ingredients, continuing to stir until everything is thoroughly combined.

Preheat the oven to 200°C/180°C fan/gas mark 6 and line a baking sheet or a 20cm x 30cm rectangular baking tin with parchment paper, depending on whether you want little oaty biscuits or flapjack-like bars. Use a teaspoon to dollop small amounts of the mixture on to a baking sheet or press the whole mixture in to the baking tin as appropriate.

Bake until golden brown – around 5-8 minutes if making biscuits on a baking sheet or around 15-20 minutes if baking in a tin. Leave to cool on the baking sheet or in the tin (allow several hours before slicing in to bars with a sharp knife). These keep for up to a week in an airtight container.

Toasted oat, date and hazelnut cookies

These chewy cookies are brilliant for kids and adults alike – they're not too sweet and taste wholesome,
a bit like a muesli bar in a cookie! Great with a glass of ice cold milk or a very strong cup of builder's tea.

MAKES 20-35

300g porridge oats
100g hazelnuts
300g refined spelt
  (or plain) flour, plus
  1 tbsp for dusting
1½ tsp baking powder
½ tsp bicarbonate
  of soda
½ tsp fine sea salt
250g unsalted butter,
  softened
200g light brown
  muscovado sugar
100g caster sugar
2 medium eggs
200g soured cream
1 tsp vanilla extract
150g chopped dates

Preheat the oven to 170°C/150°C fan/gas mark 3-4 and line two baking trays with parchment paper. You may need to bake in several batches, depending on the size of your baking trays.

Toast the oats and hazelnuts on a tray in the middle of the oven for 10 minutes, stirring halfway through so that everything toasts evenly. Remove from the oven and allow to cool slightly before skinning the hazelnuts and chopping them in halves or quarters. Leave to cool.

Stir together the flour, raising agents and salt in a medium bowl. Put the butter and the sugars in a larger bowl and cream together for about 5 minutes until pale and fluffy. Mix in the eggs, one at a time, along with a spoonful of the flour mixture each time so that the batter doesn't split.

Tip in the remainder of the flour mixture along with the soured cream, vanilla extract and the toasted oats and hazelnuts and stir through. Mix the dates in a small bowl with the extra tablespoon of flour (to stop them all clumping together), then tip in to the cookie batter and stir a few more times to distribute evenly.

Use an ice cream scoop or tablespoon to place dollops of mixture on the baking trays, leaving about 10cm between dollops so that the cookies don't merge too much. Bake in the oven for 15-20 minutes, turning the baking trays around 180° halfway through to ensure an even bake. The cookies should look pale golden in the middle and golden brown around the edges, and feel springy when you press the top. As soon as they're done, transfer to wire racks to cool.

Repeat the baking process if there is more cookie batter to use up. Allow the cookies to cool completely on a wire rack – unless, like me, you can't resist eating them while warm! These will keep in an airtight container for up to a couple of weeks. If the stored biscuits start to go soft, reheat them on a wire rack at 150°C/130°C fan/gas mark 2 for 5-10 minutes, then allow to cool completely on the wire rack once out of the oven to crisp them back up.

VARIATIONS

Why not add some spices to these cookies? Half a teaspoon of freshly grated nutmeg or a teaspoon of ground cinnamon would go particularly well.

Try using different dried fruit – sour cherries, apricots, figs, mango, raisins or sultanas – instead of the dates.

You can omit fruit altogether and add 100-150g more nuts instead – pistachios, walnuts, macadamias, pecans, Brazil nuts or almonds.

If you want to make the cookies a little more wholesome, simply substitute 75g of the refined spelt flour for wholemeal spelt, wholemeal wheat, barley, rye flour or even fine oatmeal – they're all great.

Brunostkjeks – Norwegian brown cheese biscuits

We Norwegians love our traditional brown cheese, so I'm always surprised that my beloved brunost *isn't used more often in baking, where it adds a lovely umami, salt-sweet caramel flavour. These biscuits remind me of toffee-caramel and are great on their own or sandwiched decadently around a scoop of soft vanilla ice cream. This dough freezes well, so you can always bake half now and freeze the rest to bake another day – just defrost the dough in the fridge overnight before you want to use it.*

MAKES ABOUT 30

150g plain flour
50g wholemeal flour
I tsp baking powder
¼ tsp bicarbonate of soda
¼ tsp fine sea salt
100g unsalted butter, chilled
75g *brunost* (Norwegian brown cheese)
75g brown sugar
I medium egg
I tsp vanilla extract

You can use a food processor to make this dough or mix it by hand. Combine the flours, raising agents and salt in a large bowl or food processor. Grate in the chilled butter and mix or pulse until the mixture resembles breadcrumbs.

Mix or blitz in the brown cheese and sugar, then add the egg and vanilla, mixing again until the dough comes together. Put the dough on a long sheet of clingfilm, lightly fold one side of the sheet over it and roll in the clingfilm until it forms a long sausage shape roughly 2.5-3cm in diameter. Wrap tightly in the clingfilm, twisting the ends to get it really tight and to create a uniform sausage shape, and chill in the fridge for an hour or two (or in the freezer for 20-30 minutes) until the dough feels firm to the touch.

Preheat the oven to 190°C/170°C fan/gas mark 5 and line two baking trays with baking parchment. Unwrap the dough and use a sharp knife to slice carefully in to about 30 evenly sized discs, placing them a couple of centimetres apart on the baking trays as you go. If you don't want to bake all the dough, just cut as many as you need and freeze the remaining mixture for another day.

Bake on the upper-middle shelf of the oven for 8-10 minutes until the biscuits have risen slightly and look golden brown, then cool on a wire rack. These will keep in an airtight container for up to a week. If the stored biscuits start to go soft, reheat them on a wire rack at 150°C/130°C fan/gas mark 2 for 5-10 minutes, then allow to cool completely on the wire rack once out of the oven to crisp them back up.

Joulutorttu – Finnish Christmas jam stars

These pinwheel stars are a delicious Finnish Christmas tradition. I've given them a little twist by using a spiced filling as opposed to the plain fruit centre you usually find in Finland. I make these with a cream pastry (also used for fyrstekake*), but if you prefer a flaky star then use Danish pastry dough instead. I urge you to try these even if you're not normally a prune fan – the filling tastes wonderfully of tangy spiced plums, and not at all prune-y!*

MAKES ABOUT 20-24

1 batch *fyrstekake* cream
  pastry (page 177) or
  Danish pastry dough
  (page 114)
1 cinnamon stick
3 cardamom pods
2 whole cloves
1 star anise
¼ nutmeg, freshly grated
200g soft agen prunes
juice and zest of 1 orange
juice of ½ lemon
maple syrup or soft
  brown sugar to taste
1 medium egg, beaten,
  to glaze
pearl sugar or
  sugar crystals

Follow the relevant pastry recipe up to and including chilling in the fridge for an hour (the final chilling for the Danish pastry dough before rolling).

While the pastry is chilling, wrap the spices in a muslin cloth and tie with string to create a small bag. Place the spice bag, prunes, orange juice and zest in a small saucepan, add enough water to cover the fruit and bring to a gentle simmer. Cook for 10 minutes or until the fruit has softened. Stir in the lemon juice and then taste for sweetness – if it's too acidic add a few tablespoons of maple syrup or soft brown sugar – then set aside to cool.

Line 2 baking trays with parchment paper. Roll out the pastry on a lightly floured surface or in between two sheets of baking parchment until it forms a square shape about 3mm thick, then use a sharp knife to slice in to 20-24 smaller squares of roughly equal size. Prepare each smaller square by cutting inwards from the points of the corners, slicing halfway towards the middle of the pastry. Dollop the prune filling in the uncut middle of each square and fold half of each split corner towards the middle to make a pretty jam-centred pinwheel star, sticking the pastry tips together with a little water or milk, or gently pressing the pastry tips in to the prune filling to hold them in place. It doesn't matter whether you fold in the right- or the lefthand side of the split corners, as long as you fold the same side in all the way round!

Put the stars on the baking trays. If using cream pastry, chill in the fridge for 30-45 minutes before baking. If using Danish pastry, leave to prove in a warm place for 15-20 minutes. While the stars are chilling or proving, preheat the oven to 200°C/180°C fan/gas mark 6 for cream pastry or 220°C/200°C fan/gas mark 7 for Danish pastry.

Glaze the chilled or proved stars with beaten egg and sprinkle with pearl sugar or sugar crystals. Bake for 7-9 minutes until the pastry is golden brown, keeping an eye on them after 5 minutes or so to ensure that they don't burn. Allow to cool on a wire rack before serving, as the jammy centre will be jolly hot!

Scandilicious kransekake –
baked marzipan macaroons

Kransekake *or* kransekage, *literally 'ring cake', is essentially a chewy almond macaroon and is one of my dad's favourite treats. You find it throughout Scandinavia in a variety of different shapes, from simple bars to goodie-filled horns of plenty, and of course the traditional cone-shaped pyramids constructed from stacked and glazed* kransekake *rings (hence the name) which are served at weddings, new year and other special occasions. I've adapted the classic recipe to create a chewy-crispy, utterly delicious cross between a macaroon, a tuile biscuit and a brandy snap. After they've cooled, you can drizzle the* kransekake *with white icing or chocolate, or dip their bases in dark chocolate like a florentine biscuit, but personally I like them just as they are.*

MAKES ABOUT 40-50

200g almond paste or marzipan (around 25-35% almonds)
100g whole almonds
100g icing sugar
3 medium egg whites
50g butter, melted and cooled slightly
1 tsp vanilla extract
¼ tsp fine sea salt

Preheat the oven to 200°C/180°C fan/gas mark 6 and line two baking trays with baking parchment.

Blitz the marzipan, almonds and icing sugar in a blender or food processor until they resemble breadcrumbs. Mix with all the other ingredients in a large bowl and combine to make a thick sticky mixture, bringing it together with your hands if necessary. Do be careful not to overwork or the almond oil will leach out and leave a greasy film on the biscuits. Cover with clingfilm and chill the mixture for a couple of hours or overnight.

Dollop teaspoonfuls of *kransekake* mixture on the baking trays, leaving about 6-7cm between them as they will spread when baking. You may need to bake several batches to use up all the mixture, depending on the size of your baking trays.

Bake on the upper-middle shelf of the oven for 5-8 minutes or until pale golden on top and dark golden brown on the base. Allow to cool on a wire rack. These keep well in an airtight container for a week or so, although they may start to soften after a day or two, in which case just pop them in a 160°C/140°C fan/gas mark 3 oven for a few minutes to crisp them up again. Alternatively you can store them in the freezer for up to a month (just defrost at room temperature for an hour or so before re-crisping in the oven, as above, and serving).

VARIATIONS

Add the zest of a lemon instead of, or in addition to, the vanilla extract.
Amplify the almond flavour by adding half a teaspoon of almond extract with the vanilla.
For chocolate-speckled *kransekake*, add 50g finely grated or chopped dark chocolate to the mixture.

Whisky madeleines

There are few things I find quite as satisfying as a freshly baked, crisp yet squidgy madeleine. This recipe uses barley malt extract to amplify that barley note in the whisky glaze. If you're not as much of a whisky fan as I am, substitute honey or maple syrup for the barley malt extract and use a different alcohol to glaze.

MAKES 22-24

125g unsalted butter,
  plus more for melting
2 tbsp barley
  malt extract
3 medium egg whites
125g icing sugar
50g plain flour
75g ground almonds
1 tsp baking powder
¼ tsp fine sea salt

Glaze
100g icing sugar
2-4 tbsp whisky

Melt the butter in a small saucepan over a low-medium heat and stir in the barley malt extract, allowing it to dissolve in the warm butter. Remove from the heat and set aside to cool slightly.

Whisk the egg whites and icing sugar for 5-8 minutes in a large bowl until pale and fluffy. Mix the flour, almonds, baking powder and salt in a separate bowl. Alternate between adding the dry ingredients and the malt-butter in stages, mixing as you go, until the madeleine batter looks smooth and well combined.

Cover the bowl with clingfilm and rest in the fridge overnight (or, if you're in a hurry, place in the freezer for 1 hour). Chilling the batter makes a huge difference to the crispness of the madeleines, so please don't be tempted to skip this step.

Preheat the oven to 200°C/180°C fan/gas mark 6 and brush some madeleine tins (or mini muffin tins) liberally with melted butter to stop the madeleines from sticking. Fill each indent in the greased tin(s) two-thirds full of madeleine batter. If you're baking the madeleines in several batches, put the remaining mixture back in the fridge or freezer to keep cool until needed.

Bake on the upper-middle shelf of the oven for 5-8 minutes, turning the heat down to 180°C/160°C fan/gas mark 4 after 3-4 minutes. Keep an eye on them to check that they aren't burning. The madeleines will feel springy to the touch and look pale golden in the middle with a light brown edge when they're done.

Remove from the oven and immediately use a knife (or your fingers, if you're feeling hardy) to prise the madeleines out on to a wire rack – it's much easier to remove them from the tin while they're hot. Allow to cool completely before glazing.

Mix the glaze ingredients in a small bowl – if you only want a subtle hint of whisky, use two tablespoons of whisky and two of water; otherwise use all four tablespoons of whisky. Use a pastry brush to coat the madeleines with the whisky glaze, which should be quite thick so that it doesn't run off, and allow to set for a few minutes before serving.

VARIATIONS

Use honey or maple syrup instead of barley malt and glaze with rum, Grand Marnier, chartreuse or gin icing.

If you're feeling really adventurous, how about an aniseed liqueur glaze?

Fruit liqueurs also work really well – crème de cassis, framboise, myrtilles or griotte cherry liqueur would make a delicious glaze on madeleines flavoured with honey instead of malt extract.

Lemon nutmeg madeleines

The pairing of tangy citrus and warming nutmeg in these madeleines was inspired by my mother's lemon and nutmeg krumkake *(ice cream cornet) recipe. These are light, buttery and delicious fresh from the oven. Enjoy with a cup of green or oolong tea.*

MAKES 22-24

125g unsalted butter,
  plus more for melting
2 tbsp acacia or
  other clear honey
3 medium egg whites
125g icing sugar
50g plain flour
75g ground almonds
1 tsp baking powder
zest of 1 lemon
½ nutmeg,
  freshly grated
¼ tsp fine sea salt

Glaze

100g icing sugar
zest of ½ lemon
3-4 tbsp lemon juice

Melt the butter in a small saucepan over a low-medium heat and stir in the honey, allowing it to dissolve in the warm butter. Remove from the heat and set aside to cool slightly.

Whisk the egg whites and icing sugar for 5-8 minutes in a large bowl until pale and fluffy. Mix the flour, almonds, baking powder, lemon zest, nutmeg and salt in a separate bowl. Alternate between adding the dry ingredients and the honey-butter in stages, mixing as you go, until the madeleine batter looks smooth and well combined.

Cover the bowl with clingfilm and rest in the fridge overnight (or, if you're in a hurry, place in the freezer for 1 hour). Chilling the batter makes a huge difference to the crispness of the madeleines, so please don't be tempted to skip this step.

Preheat the oven to 200°C/180°C fan/gas mark 6 and brush one or two madeleine tins (or mini muffin tins) liberally with melted butter to stop the madeleines from sticking. Fill each indent in the greased tin(s) two-thirds full of madeleine batter. If you're baking the madeleines in several batches, put the remaining mixture back in the fridge or freezer to keep cool until needed.

Bake on the upper-middle shelf of the oven for 5-8 minutes, turning the heat down to 180°C/160°C fan/gas mark 4 after 3-4 minutes. Keep an eye on them to check that they aren't burning. The madeleines will feel springy to the touch and look pale golden in the middle with a light brown edge when they're done.

Remove from the oven and immediately use a knife (or your fingers, if you're feeling hardy) to prise the madeleines out on to a wire rack – it's much easier to remove them from the tin while they're hot. Allow to cool completely before glazing.

Mix the glaze ingredients in a small bowl – the glaze should be quite thick so it doesn't run off the madeleines. Use a pastry brush to coat the madeleines with the lemon glaze and allow to set for a few minutes before serving.

VARIATIONS

Try using other citrus fruit such as orange, grapefruit, lime or clementine for the glaze.
Replace the nutmeg with a teaspoon of cinnamon or cardamom for a different twist.
Mixed spice is lovely too, giving these madeleines a distinctly Christmassy flavour.
Aniseed fans should try these with caraway, aniseed or fennel seeds in place of nutmeg.

Chocolate hazelnut brownies

I know these aren't even slightly Scandinavian but I just adore proper American brownies. As a rule of thumb with brownies, it is always better to underbake slightly rather than overbake, as they continue to cook as they cool in the tin, and I find you lose some of the intense chocolate flavour if they're overbaked. These brownies are mallowy with a flaky crust, a chewy interior, a strong hit of cocoa and just enough sweetness to balance the flavours. Irresistible.

MAKES 12

125g salted butter
75g cocoa powder
175g chocolate-hazelnut spread
2 medium eggs
2 medium yolks
150g icing sugar
50g plain flour
1 tsp vanilla extract
¼ tsp fine sea salt

Preheat the oven to 150°C/130°C fan/gas mark 2 and line a 15cm x 30cm brownie tin or a 20cm x 20cm square baking tin with two sheets of baking parchment, laid at right angles on top of each other with the ends sticking up above the edges of the tin (so that you can use the parchment to lift the brownies out of the tin after baking).

Melt the butter in a small pan, stir in the cocoa and chocolate-hazelnut spread, then set aside to cool. Lightly whisk the eggs with a fork in a medium bowl to break them up, then mix in the icing sugar until fully incorporated. Stir in the chocolate-butter mixture. Add the flour, vanilla and salt and stir a few more times – the mixture should look dark and treacly.

Pour the brownie mixture in to the prepared tin and bake on the middle shelf of the oven for 20-22 minutes – if you use a 20cm x 20cm tin it may need 2-3 minutes longer. Check the brownies after 18 minutes as they can very quickly overcook. Look for a flaky crust and a slight wobble when you shake the baking tray. If in doubt insert a skewer in the middle – there should be tiny bits of uncooked brownie mixture on it; if there are big blobs, it needs a minute or two more.

Allow to cool completely in the tin before slicing. These keep well in an airtight container for 3-4 days (although they get eaten long before then if I have anything to do with it).

VARIATIONS

If you fancy a deeper flavour, add a shot of espresso coffee with the vanilla extract. Bring out the nutty flavour in the chocolate-hazelnut spread by stirring in 50g halved or chopped toasted hazelnuts with the flour.

Norwegian chocolate rice puffs

These crispy chocolate-mocha treats were a childhood favourite of mine and make tasty teatime snacks (or retro petit fours for a dinner party!) This recipe is dairy free but you can substitute 150g butter for the coconut oil if you prefer.

MAKES 25-30

150g dark chocolate, chopped, plus more to taste
150g coconut oil
150g icing sugar, plus more to taste
I tbsp cocoa powder
I shot espresso or 2 tbsp strong coffee
I tsp vanilla extract
½ tsp fine sea salt
110g crisped rice breakfast cereal

Put the chocolate, oil, icing sugar, cocoa, coffee, vanilla and salt together in a heatproof bowl over a pan of simmering water and melt together, stirring gently. Taste the mixture and add more chocolate or icing sugar if you think it needs it.

Tip the crisped rice in to a large bowl and stir in the chocolate mixture, continuing to stir until the rice is fully coated. Spoon or scoop balls of chocolatey rice in to mini muffin or fairycake cases, or dollop on to a baking tray (make sure it fits in the fridge!)

Chill in the fridge until the chocolate sets. These will keep in the fridge for about a week, although as I find it hard to resist taking one to nibble on every time I walk past the refrigerator, they tend to disappear rather sooner than that…

VARIATION

Make these with cornflakes instead of crisped rice for another nostalgic favourite.

Romkugler – Danish rum truffles

Romkugler were invented by cunning Danish bakers who solved the problem of what to do with leftover pieces of cake by mixing the bits with jam, rum and cocoa powder to make a sweet paste, then rolling this in to balls and coating in desiccated coconut to sell afresh the next day. My recipe uses oats instead of cake crumbs, but feel free to experiment! Whether made with cake or oats, Danes will often tell you that these dark chocolatey rum truffles are one of the treats they miss most from home. I can see why, as they are utterly delicious. They are a doddle to make, so keep these in the fridge to scoff whenever you feel the need for a little pick-me-up.

MAKES 20-25

125g porridge oats
75g light brown muscovado sugar
50g unsweetened desiccated coconut, plus more for rolling
4 tbsp cocoa powder, plus more for rolling
50g coconut oil (or butter)
4 tbsp rum
4 tbsp strong coffee or a double shot espresso
¼ tsp fine sea salt

Blitz all the ingredients together in a mixer for 1-2 minutes until everything comes together like a dough. Tip the mixture on to a large sheet of clingfilm, roll up tightly in to a sausage shape, twist the clingfilm ends to seal and then refrigerate for an hour or so. It's much easier to roll the *romkugler* when the mixture is cold – if you try to roll them as soon as you've mixed everything together, things will get very messy!

Slice the chilled mixture in to 20-25 slices. Quickly roll each one in to a ball between the palms of your hands – too much rolling and they'll get warm and sticky. Roll in cocoa powder and/or desiccated coconut to coat and refrigerate until needed. These will keep well in an airtight container in the fridge for up to two weeks.

Sig's Scandi baking larder and suppliers

Here's my list of Scandi specialities and Signe favourites to help you to find some of the more unusual ingredients in this book, like my beloved Norwegian brown cheese, and also to let you know some of my preferred brands for baking ingredients. I have suggested where you might find some of these items if they aren't widely available, although in general I find that between Waitrose, IKEA, local delicatessens and websites like www.danishfooddirect. co.uk, www.totallyswedish.com and www.scandikitchen.co.uk, I can get hold of most of the ingredients needed for the recipes in this book. Other suppliers include Whole Foods Market and Planet Organic.

Abba anchovies (www.scandikitchen.co.uk)
Al Rabih pomegranate molasses (Sainsbury's, health food shops and delis)
Andreas Fine Fruit & Vegetables, London (www.andreasveg.co.uk)
Belvoir, Bottle Green or Waitrose elderflower cordial
Billington's natural sugar crystals and other sugars
Blossom Cottage cherry cordial
Chocolate by Trish cooking chocolate (www.chocolatebytrish.com or Selfridges)
Christmas cookie cutters from Lakeland (www.lakeland.co.uk)
Court Lodge Organic Bio Pouring Yoghurt (Abel & Cole)
Daim bar (Sainsbury's or www.scandikitchen.co.uk)
Dr Oetker's royal icing
Dried sour cherries (Waitrose)
Edible flowers (www.natoora.co.uk or www.msk-ingredients.com)
Forman & Son smoked salmon
Halen Môn sea salt: plain and vanilla – (www.seasalt.co.uk or Waitrose)
Hansen & Lydersen smoked salmon
Home Gourmet Factory popping candy (Waitrose)
Jarlsberg cheese (Waitrose, M&S, Sainsbury's and delis)
Jess's Ladies Organic unhomogenised whole milk (health food shops)
J.R. Feuilles de filo pastry
Kefir milk (Whole Foods Market and Planet Organic)
Kron Jäst fresh yeast (www.scandikitchen.co.uk)
L'hirondelle fresh yeast (www.thebertinetkitchen.com)
Libby's tinned pumpkin (Waitrose)
NordicWare igloo cake tin
Norwegian cod and other fresh seafood available from Direct Seafoods
  (www.directseafoods.co.uk)

O'Sheas of Knightsbridge meat (www.osheasbutchers.com)
Peter's Yard sourdough crispbread (www.petersyard.co.uk)
Rachel's Organic plain whole milk yoghurt
Riverford Organic fresh fruit and vegetables
Rococo Chocolates (www.rococochocolates.com)
Rude Health cereals, porridge and crackers
Sharpham Park spelt flour (www.sharphampark.com)
Shipton Mill spelt and other flours (www.shipton-mill.com)
Silver Spoon pectin (13g sachets)
Snøfrisk goat cheese (Waitrose and specialist suppliers)
St. Dalfour marmalades and jams
St. Ivel Cultured Buttermilk (Waitrose and other supermarkets)
Supercook edible silver balls
Tine ekte gjetost brown cheese (Waitrose and Whole Foods Market)
Trénel Fils Griotte cherry liqueur
Valrhona chocolate
Vasterbotten cheese (Waitrose)
Waitrose Canadian extra strong flour
Waitrose organic unhomogenised milk
Waitrose Ruby Grapefruit Marmalade
Willie's Cacao (Waitrose)
Yeo Valley plain whole milk yoghurt

Acknowledgements

To the Saltyard team: Publisher Elizabeth Hallett has been a dream to work with, and I owe particular thanks to Bryony Nowell, copy-editor *ne plus ultra*. Ami Smithson's ace design, Tara Fisher's beautiful photography (not to mention her black cat Jet who makes an appearance in this book!) and Annie Rigg's food styling make these baking recipes come alive, plus all of these talented ladies evinced such enthusiasm eating the food at the photo shoots, hurrah! Thanks also to Anna Hogarty, Claudette Morris, and the excellent Eleni Lawrence whose publicity skills are formidable and very much appreciated.

To Annabel Merullo for your support, and for stating my home-cured gravlaks is the best you've ever tasted, even better than in Norway. Reader, take note!

My parents Jane and Jan Johansen for being pillars of strength, love and support. I hope I can repay what you've done for me over the years. Or at least buy you dinner somewhere decent.

Tom Williams: darling Tom who never once doubted I could do this and knows when to say the right thing to soothe his irascible girlfriend, or at least proffer a snifter of whisky when needed. Thank you and all my love.

To Fiona Beckett, mentor, friend and all-star gourmet gal who shares a penchant for cardamom, a very special thank you.

To colleagues and friends who have given sound advice and encouragement, and generally been good eggs (in no particular order): Wendy Wilson Bett, Ian and Christina Tencor and the Peter's Yard team, Tim Hayward, Niamh Shields, Linda Williams, Ailbhe Phelan, Trine Hahnemann, Elly Cushens, Mat Couchman, Denise Medrano, Maunika Gowardhan, Sabrina Ghayour, Petra Barran, Kerstin Rodgers, Shayma Sadaat, Donna D, Keiko Oikawa, James Ramsden, Lucy Pope, Camilla and Nick Barnard at Rude Health, Bronte and Jonas Aurell at the Scandi Kitchen, Alison Lea-Wilson at Halen Mon, John Lister at Shipton Mill, Richard Bertinet, Simon Majumdar, Dino Joannides, Andreas Georghiou, Daniel and Vivien Young, Matt Inwood, Toni Horton at Something, Britta Gertsen and Rococo, Magnus Englund at Skandium, Sarah Canet, Richard Ehrlich, Silvija Davidson, Richard Turner, Huw Gott, Will Beckett, Lorraine Pascale, Dan Lepard, Russell Norman, Chris at the Real Bread Campaign, Harry West, Fraser and Lynda Reid, Mette and Egil *Austbø*, Elin Prangerod at Norseland, Ailana Kamelmacher, thank you one and all. Takk til tante Randi og onkel Øystein.

Thank you for your recipe suggestions Tine Roche at the Cambridge Cookery School, Eleonoora Kirk, Hanne Stensvold, and to Kenwood UK for the awesome Kenwood mixer.

To friends from Cambridge, SOAS, Leiths, et al., you know who you are x

This book is dedicated in memoriam to my grandmothers Juliet Robertson-Macdonald and Oddny Solveig Vikesland Johansen, both fantastic bakers. I wish I could share this with them, even though I know my bread-making hands will never produce as crisp, light and tender pastry as these two bakers made. I hope this book does justice to their superlative baking and everything they taught in the kitchen.

Last but not least, thank you dear reader for buying, blagging or borrowing this book. May it take pride of place in your kitchen for years to come! Sig x

Index

Page references in **bold** indicate photographs

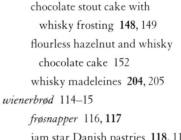

First published in Great Britain in 2012 by Saltyard Books
An imprint of Hodder & Stoughton
An Hachette UK company

ISBN 978 1 444 73467 6

Typeset in Granjon, Baskerville and Mrs Eaves
Design by www.cabinlondon.co.uk
Food and props stylist Annie Rigg
Copy-editor Bryony Nowell
Proofreader Margaret Gilby
Indexer Caroline Wilding

Colour reproduction by FMG
Printed and bound in China by C&C Offset Printing Co. Ltd

Hodder & Stoughton policy is to use papers that are natural,
renewable and recyclable products and made from wood grown in sustainable forests.
The logging andmanufacturing processes are expected to conform to the environmental
regulations of the country of origin.

Hodder & Stoughton Ltd
338 Euston Road London
NW1 3BH

www.saltyardbooks.co.uk